D0856889

Quotations from the Anarchists

QUOTATIONS

·

FROM THE

·

ANARCHISTS

EDITED BY PAUL BERMAN

PRAEGER PUBLISHERS
New York · Washington · London

PRAEGER PUBLISHERS
111 Fourth Avenue, New York, N.Y. 10003, U.S.A.
5, Cromwell Place, London SW7 2JL, England

Published in the United States of America in 1972
by Praeger Publishers, Inc.

Library of Congress Catalog Card Number: 74–173275

Printed in the United States of America

CONTENTS

·

88024

The following publishers and authors granted permission to excerpt from their published works:

E. J. Brill, publisher, of Leiden, Netherlands, for *Archives Bakounine,* edited by Arthur Lehning, A. J. C. Rüter, and P. Scheibert, three volumes, 1961–1965.

Dover Publications, New York, for their reprints of *God and the State,* by Michael Bakunin, 1970; *Anarchism and Other Essays,* by Emma Goldman, 1969; *Kropotkin's Revolutionary Pamphlets,* by Peter Kropotkin, edited by Roger Baldwin, 1970; *What Is Property?* by Pierre-Joseph Proudhon, translation by Benj. R. Tucker, 1970.

The Macmillan Company, New York, for *The Political Philosophy of Bakunin: Scientific Anarchism,* edited by G. P. Maximoff, © The Free Press, 1953.

E. H. Carr, for his book *Michael Bakunin,* copyright 1937 by The Macmillan Company.

The Freedom Press, London, for *Marxism, Freedom, and the State,* by Michael Bakunin, edited by K. J. Kenafick, 1950; *Malatesta: Life and Ideas,* edited by Vernon Richards, 1965; and *Lessons of the Spanish Revolution,* by Vernon Richards, 1953. The last two works are quoted by the kind permission of Vernon Richards.

Marquette University Press, Milwaukee, Wisc., for *The Doctrine of Anarchism of Michael A. Bakunin,* by Eugene Pyziur, 1955.

Schocken Books, New York, for its reprints of *Prison Memoirs of an Anarchist,* by Alexander Berkman, 1970; *The Great French Revolution* and *In Russian and French Prisons,* by Peter Kropotkin, 1971.

Ian Ballantine, for *Living My Life,* by Emma Goldman, published by Alfred A. Knopf, Inc., 1931; and *My Disillusionment in Russia,* by Emma Goldman, reprinted by Thomas Y. Crowell, 1970.

The M.I.T. Press, for *Selected Writings on Anarchism and Revolution,* by Peter Kropotkin, edited by Martin A. Miller, 1970.

Cambridge University Press, for *The Spanish Labyrinth,* by Gerald Brenan, 1964.

François Maspero, Paris, for *Ni Dieu Ni Maître,* by Daniel Guérin, 1970.

Doubleday and Company, Inc., for *Selected Writings of P.-J. Proudhon,* edited by Stewart Edwards and translated by Elizabeth Fraser, 1969.

Secker and Warburg, London, for *Anarcho-Syndicalism,* by Rudolf Rocker, 1938.

Chilton Book Company, Philadelphia, for *After the Revolution,* by D. A. de Santillan. Copyright © 1937 by Greenberg, Publisher, Inc. Reprinted by permission of Chilton Book Company, Philadelphia.

Henry David, for *The History of the Haymarket Affair,* by Henry David, Farrar and Rinehart, 1936. By permission of the author.

Quotations from the Anarchists

EDITOR'S INTRODUCTION

The modern socialist casting about for historical perspective may well imagine that socialism is necessarily centralist and statist, invariably grounded on some degree of hierarchy and authority, leadership and rigid control. These factors are evident in all socialist governments today and in many of the organizations on the Left. But there are other traditions of socialism too.

Anarchism, anti-state and anti-authoritarian, is the second great current in the socialist movement. Anarchism was the dominant tendency in the First International for a number of years, in the infancy of the movement. Such Anarchists as Pierre-Joseph Proudhon and Michael Bakunin were better known than their rivals Karl Marx and Frederick Engels. The labor movements in France, Italy, Spain, and other countries were pioneered by Anarchists. Yet Anarchism, as an organized, libertarian socialist movement, has all but disappeared. Or has it?

The revival of Anarchism is part of a general resurgence of interest in libertarian opposition, an opposition made possible, it might be argued, by the social achievement of industrial wealth and made desirable by the pervasive influence of authoritarian industrial forms in political and social life. Certainly, libertarian ideals are not foreign to Marxism; a number of Marxist movements have emphasized these elements of Marx's own writings, especially in the last few years. But libertarian ideals inherent to Marxism are easily obscured, lost in historical practice, overwhelmed by the authoritarian principles of centralism, elitism, and hierarchical discipline. Against the historically preponderant authoritarian form that Marxism has taken in this century, Anarchism poses an alternative historical tradition, because concepts of individual liberty, self-activity, and nonhierarchical forms of organization are the very bases of its thought.

"Anarchism," wrote the Italian revolutionary Errico Malatesta, "was born of a moral revolt to social injustice." It is essentially grounded on a moral opposition and ethos. The Anarchists are "rebels at all hours," a French comrade boasted, "men truly without God, without master and without country, irreconcilable enemies of all despotisms, moral or material, individual or collective." To such men and women, revolution is a felt necessity, a moral imperative rather than a historical inevitability. Some Anarchists reject the perspective of a particular class to embrace that of all the oppressed, asserting that revolution is a willful act of all those who are revolted and unsoiled by the morality of the status quo. Revolution is made by the workers, yes, but also by the peasants, the rebellious "lumpenproletariat" at the bottom of society, the idealistic youth, and the déclassé intellectuals with no future in the bourgeois framework.

"Evil, in the eyes of the Anarchists," Peter Kropotkin told his trial judges in 1883, ". . . is in the principle of authority." Libertarianism defines the moral passion of Anarchism, and indeed, the elaboration of a radical thrust inherent in classical liberalism provides the root of much Anarchist thought and insight. "I am a fanatic lover of liberty," proclaimed his Russian countryman Michael Bakunin, "considering it as the unique condition under which intelligence, dignity, and the happiness of men can develop and grow; not that purely formal liberty, conceded, measured, and regulated by the State, an eternal lie and which in reality never represents anything but the privilege of the few founded on the slavery of everyone, not that individualist, shabby, and fictional liberty proclaimed by the . . . schools of bourgeois liberty. . . .

No, I mean the only liberty truly worthy of the name, liberty that consists in the full development of all the powers—material, intellectual, and moral—that are latent faculties of each; liberty that recognizes no other restrictions than those outlined for us by the laws of our own individual nature, so that properly speaking, there are no restrictions. . . .

I mean that liberty of each individual which, far from halting as at a boundary before the liberty of others, finds there its confirmation and its extension to infinity; the illimitable liberty of each through the liberty of all, liberty by solidarity, liberty in equality; liberty triumphing over brute force and the principle of authority that was never anything but the intellectualized expression of that force; liberty which, after having overthrown all heavenly and earthly idols, will found and organize a new world, that of human solidarity, on the ruins of all Churches and all States.[1]

The individual is the Anarchist's center of society. In his or her interest, social relations of domination and servility must be repudiated, for they degrade the one and deprave the other. The replacement of these relations with free ones is the essence of positive social development; the freedom of the individual is the touchstone of progress.

Anarchist opposition to capitalism is based, then, not on historical analysis but on the ideal of liberty. Capitalism destroys liberty through the control and exploitation of the many by the few—the owners or capitalists. Similarly, the hierarchical industrial system itself is destructive to the individual, to what Bakunin called the "full development" of his or her powers. It is founded on specialization, on hierarchy, on uniformity and monotony, imposed discipline, and inculcated resignation. The worker is powerless, stripped of all autonomy. "Man is being robbed not merely of the products of his labor," the American Anarchist Emma Goldman objected, "but [also] of the power of free initiative, of originality. . . . Strange to say, there are people who extol this deadening method of centralized production as the proudest achievement of our age. They fail utterly to realize that if we are to continue in machine subserviency, our slavery is more complete than was our bondage to the King."[2]

The State, too, is a block to freedom. "Royalty, or the government of man by man, is illegitimate and absurd," wrote the young Proudhon in his pioneering tract *What Is Property?* (the answer to which is "theft"). The State is domination institutionalized, carried to its inevitable and violent extreme by its indispensable arsenal of armies, prisons, and police. Considered as the expression of the popular will, "the State is an abstraction devouring the life of the people," in Bakunin's words. No matter what its justification may be—divine right or popular mandate—the State is nothing more than a powerful minority ruling and therefore oppressing the powerless majority. It is an elite, with interests different from those of the people. In the interests of its own welfare, the State must always expand its despotism, internally as repression and externally as conquest. It matters little whether this elite is chosen by ballots, birth, or blows, for it is the nature of any elite—"public servants" or capitalist masters—to oppress and exploit those whom it controls.

By rejecting every State as hostile to the people, Anarchists rejected the idea of a revolutionary government as well. The two terms, revolution and government, are in fact mutually exclusive, since the goal of the revolution is to secure liberty and the goal of the State is to curb it. This repudiation of the State and of all elites as potential agents of revolution was the chief issue that split the European socialist movement down the middle. A century ago, in 1872, the International Workingmen's Association—the First International—broke apart over the mud-slinging but historically crucial debate between Bakunin, bombastic spokesman of the "anti-authoritarian" wing, and Karl Marx, dominant intellect of the "authoritarians." For Marx, social revolution implied that the working class must become the ruling class, by seizing and utilizing State power; his close collaborator Engels added that this new State would ultimately "wither away" after the triumph of socialism. Flamboyant Bakunin —at that time more renowned for his exploits and colossal energy in revolutionary action than the scholarly and less obtrusive Marx—polemicized against Statist revolution. Although Bakunin distorted Marx's later position, he clearly outlined the nature of some later revolutions. "What does it mean, the proletariat elevated to a ruling class?" he asked. "There are about forty million Germans. Are all forty million going to be members of the government? The whole people will govern and no one will be governed. There will be no government and no State; but if there is a State, people will be governed and there will be slaves." Nor can this tyranny of the ruling elite be prevented by universal suffrage. Elections might return workers to the government, Bakunin argued, but he added that these elected workers would be only "*former* workers, perhaps, who as soon as they become rulers or representatives of the people will cease to be workers and will start viewing the worker's world from the heights of the State; they will no longer represent the people, but only themselves and their pretensions to rule the people. Anyone who doubts this is just not familiar with the nature of man."[3] He predicted a "new class, a new hierarchy" of bureaucrats and intellectuals. Such a State will never wither away. "No dictatorship can have any goal but self-perpetuation. . . . Freedom can only be created by freedom."

Anarchists want to destroy State power, not seize it. Freedom must have a social form, of course, but Anarchists propose one altogether different from hierarchy and the State. Freedom, in the Anarchist sense, exists only when individuals —even (and especially) associated together in groups—consciously guide their personal and societal lives. Only when they govern themselves can individuals emerge as individuals, not bound together by a common tyranny, not separated from one another by extreme specialization of functions or by loss of control over their own products and production. To the Anarchist, individualization is the essence of freedom, and self-management is the basis for a free society.

In search of nontyrannical social and economic arrangements, theoreticians like Kropotkin tended to look to the free artisan—industrious and independent, creative in his labor, united with his fellow-workers—and to the rounded independence and communism of idealized peasant life, disdained by Marx as "the idiocy of rural life." Rather than advocate a return to obsolete social forms, most Anarchists took these idealizations as models for social and industrial reorganization and insisted that, in the spirit of these nonindustrial forms, the free individual in socialist society requires self-management and the abolition of a separate class of managers. Bakunin, Malatesta, and the Anarcho-syndicalists (Anarchist trade unionists) never questioned the need for industrial centralization but emphasized that it must be based on self-management.

The critical institution of Anarchy, a society without a ruler, is the local assembly, the free association of individuals for mutual aid and collective action. Freely generated and disbanded, such assemblies are a full and direct democracy, reaching decisions by consensus and free experimentation but not by the tyranny of the majority. The basic economic organization is the workers' council, the local assembly in the fields as in the factory, shop, and store. Similarly, neighborhood and local political and social groupings would form communes administered by free assemblies. Totally accountable and instantly recallable delegates would unite the various councils and communes into a series of broader federations—industrial, agricultural, regional, and national. The federations would aid, share, coordinate, and even economically centralize, but they would have no existence outside the local assemblies, nor would there be any form of political centralism; the right of secession is paramount and indisputable. Power would remain decentralized, in each council and commune. "The idea of a council system for labor," the German union organizer Rudolf Rocker wrote, "is the practical overthrow of the State as a whole. It stands, therefore, in frank antagonism to any form of dictatorship, which must always have in view the highest development of the power of the State."[4]

The Anarchist thus no more advocates chaos than does the strictest authoritarian; but the Anarchist seeks order in diversity and agreement rather than in uniformity and control. Moreover, order consists in change; a free society cannot be static. It must form a fluid organism, a natural unity that, left unhampered, freely adjusts and grows in the face of new requirements and aspirations. Anarchy is incompatible with constricting social forms or rigid and dogmatic thought. "Our most vivid imaginations cannot foresee the potentialities of a race set free from restraint," Emma Goldman wrote. "We, who pay dearly for every breath of pure, fresh air, must guard against the tendency to fetter the future."

The freedom of self-management exists only where it is self-gained, self-proclaimed, and self-maintained. Anarchists reject the principle of political representation and assert that if power and freedom are delegated, they simply become the power and freedom of someone else; the self-management of the people cannot be administered by some bureaucracy or elite. Likewise, liberation must be achieved by direct action. Long after the split in the First International, Anarchists retained Marx's slogan for that organization: "The emancipation of the working class is the task of the workers themselves." They expressly denied Lenin's contention that a guiding elite, a "vanguard of the proletariat," was required to self-assertedly represent the people. "One thing is indisputable," the aged Kropotkin wrote to Lenin in 1920, "even if the dictatorship of the party were an appropriate means to bring about a blow to the capitalist system (which I strongly doubt), it is nevertheless harmful for the creation of a new socialist system." Anarchists remain among the people. "If we believe that it is sufficient to overthrow the government, then we will become an army of conspirators," Kropotkin stated some years earlier, "but we . . . do not conceive of the revolution in this way.

> The next revolution must from its inception bring about the seizure of the entire social wealth by the workers in order to transform it into common property. This revolution can succeed only through the workers, only if the urban and rural workers carry out this objective themselves. . . . The revolutionary bourgeoisie can overthrow the government, but it cannot make the revolution; this only the people can do.[5]

The role of the Anarchists, then, is to help the people to organize, inform them, and urge them to revolution. Bakunin advocated a disciplined and tightly organized international underground. Most Anarchists, however, favored decentralized and libertarian groups. "An Anarchist organization must, in my opinion," Malatesta counseled, "[allow] complete autonomy and independence, and therefore full responsibility, to individuals and groups." Instead of building strength through centralism and hierarchical control, Anarchists based it on the complementary principles of solidarity and autonomy, libertarian and socialist values.

These values are in fact the essence of Anarchist revolution. This revolution, Kropotkin wrote, "is not, as has sometimes been said by those indulging in metaphysical wooliness, just a question of giving the worker 'the total product of his labor'; it is a question of completely reshaping all relationships." Indeed, it is social and human values themselves that must be transformed, for, lacking that, the revolution would be "a change of form only," Goldman explained in 1922, "not of substance, as [was] so tragically proved by Russia." A change in substance must be consciously brought about, it must be created out of its opposite. Conscious revolutionaries should begin or aid the process by transforming themselves to reflect the new values. "The surest means of making Anarchism triumph," wrote the French militant Jean Grave, "is to act as an Anarchist."

"The Anarchists are distinguished from the other schools of socialist thought," Luis Mercier-Vega observed, "by the fact that they judge society as a whole and oppose to it a counter-society." "Acting as an Anarchist" is the first step in the creation of a "counter-society." Anarchist groups scrupulously avoided bureaucracies and elite leaderships and stressed the freedom of the individual. Some remarkably strong and devoted personalities developed out of these experiences; militants like Malatesta spent a lifetime—in his case, some sixty-odd years of virtually continuous agitation—reflecting their revolutionary principles in everyday life, maintaining their individuality, and refusing oppressive roles.

But while libertarian values sustained the character of the movement, some Anarchists evolved into a breed apart, characterized by an intense morality and quasi-religious zeal of little relevance to the agitational and organizational needs of radical activity. Ideological partiality to individualism and rebelliousness sometimes produced moral strength and sometimes sustained a disruptive chaos. The labor movement's desertion of radicalism in the last two decades of the nineteenth century isolated the Anarchists and further inflamed the worst of their tendencies. With little support and little activity in most of Europe, the movement developed along the lines of sheer wishful thinking and isolated, ineffectual moral protest. Inspired by the futuristic idylls of Kropotkin and others, some Anarchists formed small, congenial, liberated life-style colonies. Some individuals, occasionally on the borders of the movement and often on the borders of bearable frustration, took lone actions against the State and the bourgeoisie. Over a span of twenty years, Anarchist terrorists assassinated the monarchs of Austria and Italy, the Presidents of France and the United States, the Prime Minister of Spain, and a host of lesser dignitaries. Russian populists assassinated the Czar. Except for the assassination of the Czar, these instances of "propaganda by the deed" were isolated acts by isolated people claiming to represent an isolated movement. The masses were unmoved, if not disgusted, but the various states involved were stirred indeed. Political repression resulted in mass trials and imprisonments; captured terrorists, and sometimes nonterrorists too, were executed one after another. Other terrorist acts randomly directed at the bourgeoisie as a whole did not fail to produce results even more devastating to the movement. Moreover, the Anarchist movement as a whole was unable to repudiate these acts of a few individuals, lest it compromise its support of individual initiative.

If individual violence and fatalist optimism marked a low point of the Anarchist movement, the positive significance of Anarchism was marked by the resurgence at the end of the century of an Anarchist labor movement, dormant in most of Europe since the collapse of the First International. Anarcho-syndicalism was the idea of a "counter-society" extended to the working class as a whole. Like the other Anarchist currents, Anarcho-syndicalism was anti-Statist and anti-parliamentary. Certainly, Anarchist unions sought to better working conditions, but not through the power of the polls or by influence over politicians. Anarcho-syndicalists supported direct action—forms of struggle like strikes, boycotts, and sabotage—both as a means of securing temporary amelioration and ultimately as a means of making the social revolution. "What is important," the Spanish Anarcho-syndicalist

Abad de Santillan wrote, just before his country's civil war, ". . . is to create the organism which will have to solve the daily and immediate problems of the Revolution. This organism, we believe, can be no other than organized labor, without intervention of the State and without intermediaries and parasites." The Anarcho-syndicalist union plants the seeds of socialism in its own practice, preparing itself to be the actual basis of the social organization of the future. Conforming to Anarchist principles, the union resists the tendency to create an elite leadership and a bureaucracy. Each shop and factory committee is autonomous, united by a strong sense of solidarity and by a federal structure.

Anarcho-syndicalism was the most successful form of Anarchism. Although its ascendancy lasted only two or three decades, strong Anarcho-syndicalist unions existed at one time or another throughout Europe, in Latin America, and in China; their strongest roots of all were in Spain. Anarchism was inaugurated there in 1868 by a delegate of Bakunin's organization, the Alliance of Social Democracy; Bakunin contentedly wrote that "the demon of social revolution has taken firm possession of Spain." Despite the rival proselytizing of Marx's son-in-law, and subsequent more serious clashes with the Marxist movement, Spanish workers remained largely Anarchist. Anarchism grew through a series of organizations and uprisings, outlawings and brutal repressions. The Anarcho-syndicalist National Confederation of Labor (CNT) was formed in 1910 and acquired hundreds of thousands of members among low-skilled industrial workers and poor peasants and farm workers. The largest and most militant socialist organization in the country, the CNT was assiduously courted by Lenin's Third International, formed after the Russian Revolution. The CNT pledged support. But in 1922, after news reached Spain of the repression of the Ukrainian Anarchists and of Trotsky's brutal suppression of the revolutionary proletariat of "Red Kronstadt," the Anarcho-syndicalists broke with the Communist movement.

Because of the high level of Anarchist consciousness and the savagery of class war in Spain, the CNT retained its revolutionary vitality through the years of severe repression and underground organization. Despite its enormous size, it developed no bureaucracy; there was only one paid official, and the organization was sustained by the workers. It normally shunned government elections, on the rare occasions when these took place; its power developed independently. Gerald Brenan recounts how in the rural villages the "local syndicates [unions] everywhere acquired immense prestige and authority. . . . The municipality kept only a nominal power. Every Sunday the syndicate would meet in full assembly to discuss local affairs. The whole village attended and anyone who wished had a right to speak." Voting was by show of hands, and the committee that was elected enforced its will by fines that could be appealed at the next weekly meeting.[6]

With the world capitalist depression of 1929 and the restoration of republican rule in Spain two years later, the Anarchists mounted a series of general strikes and uprisings, although the issues were more often political than material. In 1934, for example, the heavily Anarchist working class of Saragossa declared a general strike on two demands: to restore the suspended licenses of a group of local bus drivers and to free political prisoners taken in an earlier insurrection. The bus drivers' licenses were soon restored, but the strike continued for almost six weeks in support of the prisoners. When General Franco's forces attempted a rightist military *coup* in July, 1936, the high level of working-class consciousness precipitated a revolution. In nearly every major city in the country, the military insurrection was countered, not by the faltering government, but by the armed and organized workers.

The attempted fascist *coup* was thrown back within a few days. A general strike paralyzed the national economy, and the workers began systematic expropriation of industry, agriculture, public utilities, shops, hotels, and businesses, even the homes of the wealthy. Economic reorganization began rapidly, in the form of collectivization under the direct management of the workers. Committees were formed in the seized factories, and organizations such as the food-workers' union in Catalonia administered to basic needs. Through the CNT and the Socialist unions (UGT), local unions and workers' committees federated together on local and then on regional lines to facilitate production and distribution. Falteringly at first, the economy once more began to function in most areas of unoccupied Spain.

The urban revolution was most profound in Barcelona. Franz Borkenau, an observer unsympathetic to Anarchism, described the expropriation in that city from his experiences there in August, 1936:

> The amount of expropriation in the few days since 19 July is almost incredible. The largest hotels, with one or two exceptions, have all been requisitioned by working-class organizations (not burnt, as had been reported . . .). So were most of the larger stores. . . . Practically all the factory owners . . . had either fled or been killed and their factories taken over by the workers. Everywhere large posters at the front of impressive buildings proclaim the fact of expropriation, explaining either that the management is now in the hands of the CNT or that a particular organization has appropriated the building for its organizing work.[7]

Another observer, the English writer and journalist George Orwell, arrived in Barcelona four months later. He found the city in "a state of affairs worth fighting for" and described it in *Homage to Catalonia:*

> It was the first time that I had ever been in a town where the working class was in the saddle. . . . Every shop and café had an inscription saying that it had been collectivized; even the bootblacks had been collectivized and their boxes painted red and black [the colors of the Anarcho-syndicalists]. Waiters and shopwalkers looked you in the face and treated you as an equal.

Servile and even ceremonial forms of speech had temporarily disappeared. . . . There were no private motor-cars, they had all been commandeered, and all the trams and taxis and much of the other transport were painted red and black. . . . Practically everyone wore rough working-class clothes or blue overalls or some variant of the militia uniform. All this was queer and moving. . . .

Above all, there was a belief in the revolution and the future, a feeling of having suddenly emerged into an era of equality and freedom. Human beings were trying to act as human beings and not as cogs in the capitalist machine. In the barbers' shops were Anarchist notices (the barbers were mostly Anarchists) solemnly explaining that barbers were no longer slaves.

The labor unions formed militia units, while other workers stayed at their jobs in the factories. H. E. Kaminski, a French libertarian writer also in Catalonia, reported after his tour of industrial plants that "the work is as good or better than before, in the war industries as much as fourteen hours a day without overtime pay. The workers consider the factories as their property and take care of them with a jealous vanity." In spite of a critical shortage of raw materials and the loss of large markets in fascist-occupied Spain, the factory and industrial committees began the difficult task of industrial centralization and were able to convert some plants to armaments manufacture. Kaminski spent several hours in the largest textile factory in Spain, with 1,800 employees. "The directors have remained as technicians," he wrote, "and despite the revolution they draw a slightly larger pay than the other workers." Nevertheless, "the management proper is in the hands of the factory council, composed of nineteen workers and employees elected by the personnel." By not paying the large salaries of the former capitalist management, the plant had reduced expenses by 13 per cent. The factory council members received workers' pay.

Women workers were not represented on the council: This was the major failing in this experiment in workers' control,

although none of the men or women workers Kaminski
spoke to seemed to find it objectionable. However, there was
day-care service for children under six, and mothers had time
off in the morning and afternoon to be with their children.

> As to questions of improvements that they wanted [Kaminski
> observed], one always received the same general and vague
> responses: liberty for all, socialism, fraternity. . . . They are
> all, with a few exceptions, in favor of a uniform salary for
> everyone, corresponding to the Anarchist ideas.
>   There is not the least doubt about the revolutionary con-
> victions of these men and women workers. The men are volun-
> tarily forging scrap metal that they find in the factory in order
> to use it for the war.[8]

While the industrial workers achieved extraordinary suc-
cesses in workers' control, Anarchism, or libertarian communism, was actually most successful among the poor peasants and farm workers. Rural collectivization is often the
nemesis of centrally directed revolutions, but in Spain it was
the culminating work of fifty years of Anarchist agitation.
Collectivization was spontaneous in wide areas, generally
among the poorest peasants. General assemblies of working
peasants in each village elected management committees for
the administration of the collectivized property—which often
as not consisted of the entire wealth of the village. On the
theory that socialism must be voluntary, small individual
landholders and small traders were usually not coerced into
joining the collectives, although they often joined later because of the social and economic inducements.
  Rural expropriation and collectivization proceeded on a
massive scale. Total confiscations ultimately accounted for
more than a third of the arable land in the regions unoccupied by the fascists, a larger amount than that achieved in
the original Russian Revolution and civil war of 1917 to
1921. In Catalonia, the zeal of the peasants, many of them
small landowners, did not match that of the urban workers,

and the number of collectives was relatively small. But in Aragon province, more than three-quarters of the land was seized by hundreds of collectives with almost a half million members. Massive collectivization also occurred in the Valencia region, in Castile, and in Estremadura and Andalusia, two provinces where the Anarchist tradition was strong but which fell to the fascists early in the war. Crop production generally increased under collectivization, and this can be credited to the effective organization of the countryside. Local communes united into cantonal federations, and these in turn united in regional federations. Solidarity between villages, "equalization funds" between rich villages and poor ones, and the studies of agronomists and agricultural technicians also boosted efficiency. A level of solidarity was also maintained between the rural and urban workers, a rare feat in the history of social revolutions.

These facts and statistics are impressive, but perhaps the most astounding achievements of the Spanish Revolution were in the application of Anarchist social ideals. "We want to reconstruct Spain both materially and morally," proclaimed the Iberian Anarchist Federation (FAI). "Our revolution will be both economic and ethical." And, indeed, many of the rural villages inaugurated Anarchist ethics from the beginning of the revolution. In an essay on "Objectivity and Liberal Scholarship," Noam Chomsky quotes a 1937 CNT study of collectivization in which the village of Membrilla is described. Eight thousand people lived there in miserable huts, without a newspaper, movie theater, café, or library. There was an abundance of churches, however, and these had been burned. The land had been expropriated, and village life was collectivized. Money was abolished; work and consumption were socialized (communalized). "It was, however," the CNT report noted, "not a socialization of wealth but of poverty." An elected council regulated the life of the commune and administered the free distribution of the available necessities of life. The account closes with these words:

The whole population lived as in a large family; functionaries, delegates, the secretary of the syndicates, the members of the municipal council, all elected, acted as heads of a family. But they were controlled, because special privilege or corruption would not be tolerated. Membrilla is perhaps the poorest village in Spain, but it is the most just.[9]

Likewise, Franz Borkenau visited the village of Castro, "a typically populous and wretched Andalusian *pueblo*. ... The salient point of the Anarchist regime in Castro is the abolition of money," he reported. "The committee took over the estates and runs them," but not very efficiently in this case. "Money wages, of course, have been abolished. It would be incorrect to say that they have been replaced by pay in kind. There is no pay whatever; the inhabitants are fed directly from the village stores." Similarly, the small town of Fraga in Aragon boasted of its revolution in an Anarchist newspaper: "Here in Fraga you can throw banknotes into the street and no one will take any notice. Rockefeller, if you were to come to Fraga with your entire bank account, you would not be able to buy a cup of coffee. Money, your God and your servant, has been abolished here, and the people are happy."[10] In villages where money was not entirely abolished, standard wages were replaced by the "family wage," which varied according to the size of the family.

Gaston Leval, a French Anarchist, concluded that the Spanish revolution "is the first time in modern society that the Anarchist principle 'to each according to his needs' has been practiced."[11] Writing while the war against Franco was still in progress, Rudolf Rocker added that the Spanish working class has

proved that the workers, even without the capitalists, are able to carry on production and do it better than a lot of profit-hungry entrepreneurs. Whatever the outcome of the bloody war in Spain may be, to have given this great demonstration remains the indisputable service of the Spanish Anarcho-syndicalists, whose heroic example has opened up for the Socialist movement new outlooks for the future.

The workers lost the war, but they lost the revolution first. With the Franco insurgency, the government all but disintegrated, and the antifascist middle classes were left unable to prevent a social revolution made by the same workers who were their only bulwark against fascism. But eventually, a capable party stepped forward to strengthen the government and lead the middle and lower middle classes, a party that, moreover, controlled the sole significant source of foreign military aid. This was the Communist Party of Spain, under direct orders from the Moscow Comintern, whose interest lay in defeating the social revolution as well as fascism, to avoid arousing the hostility of capitalist countries against Soviet Russia.

"Russian intervention," Gerald Brenan records, "gave the Communists a position that they could never otherwise have held in Spain.

The power to distribute the arms that arrived put the Anarchists in their hands. . . . Unable to draw to themselves the manual workers, who remained fixed in their [Anarcho-syndicalist and Socialist] unions, the Communists found themselves the refuge for all those who had suffered from the excesses of the Revolution or who feared where it might lead them. Well-to-do Catholic orange-growers in Valencia, peasants in Catalonia, small shopkeepers and businessmen, Army officers and government officials enrolled in their ranks. . . . There were even a few rich manufacturers who obtained important posts in it [the Party].[12]

The Communist Party used its new power and social bases effectively against the Revolution. Although the Party itself fought heroically against the fascists, it also denied arms to the Anarchist troops at the Aragon front and similarly inhibited Socialist troops attempting to liberate Estremadura. Perhaps most important in defeating the revolution was the brutal Communist suppression of Anarchist and other extreme-left groups and the seizure, in the name of the government, of collectivized industry and agriculture, destroying workers' control. In some instances, factories and lands were returned to their original private owners; elsewhere, the Communist-dominated bureaucracy took over from the workers' committees and restored the workers to their former position of subservience. Demoralization was intense, and the blow to the war effort was considerable.

If the Spanish Bolsheviks were successful counterrevolutionaries, the Spanish Anarchists were equally unsuccessful revolutionaries. Why did they fail? First, they confronted probably insuperable odds. Second, the Anarchists were unable to abolish the State because they were unable to render it useless, not even by constructing a strongly coordinated social organism built, on Bakunin's specifications, "from the bottom to the top and from the circumference to the center, conforming to the principle of liberty." Many Anarchists, the Spanish included, favored federal centralization of the economy. But Anarchist thinking rejects anything that smacks of political centralism, and the Spanish Anarchists were unable to coordinate their military and civil administration tightly enough to defeat the counterrevolution. Ultimately, the Anarchists themselves joined the State in a futile effort to restrain the antirevolutionary forces. They had no other defense.

By 1939, Anarchism no longer represented a significant organized radical movement in any country. Everywhere its mass following gravitated toward the Communist parties, and historians and rival Leftists gladly consigned it to the tomb. But if the collapse of the Anarchist movement represented the ultimate victory of Marx over Bakunin, it was a mixed triumph indeed. As a prophet of revolution, it is Bakunin who deserves the greater recognition. Revolution in our century has occurred not in the most advanced countries but in the nonindustrial world, among peasants and low-skilled workers. The works of Fanon, Paul Avrich has noted, sometimes read as if taken word for word from the pages of Bakunin. Moreover, the triumphs of State socialism have everywhere, to varying degrees, realized Bakunin's predictions of a "new class," a despotic bureaucracy that will never wither away.

More important, Anarchist ideas and social forms tend to spring up spontaneously during social revolutions, with or without active Anarchist agitation. The principles of Anarchist social organization, Kropotkin wrote, "already dated from 1789, and . . . they had their origin, not in theoretic speculations, but in the *deeds* of the Great French Revolution," in the local "districts" and "sections" of revolutionary Paris, and in the local communes of provincial France that largely powered the upheaval. In the more modern Mexican and Russian revolutions, Anarchist movements spontaneously arose among peasants. It is interesting to observe that the village structure of the Vietnamese National Liberation Front is based on a high degree of syndicalist-like direct democracy and self-management, called "people's self-rule" by Vietnamese writers.

Self-management and workers' control in the form of workers' councils also characterized the spontaneous organization of urban and industrial workers in revolutions in Italy and Germany after World War I, as well as in Russia before the triumph of the party bureaucracy and in Spain. Although peasant Anarchism may have little relevance to modern industrial societies, workers' councils and factory committees as bases of social organization persist as a spontaneous alternative to bureaucratic socialism. In this sense, the contemporary revival of libertarian socialism might be dated from the Hungarian workers' revolution of 1956, in which factory committees and free trade unions battled the State bureaucracy and foreign occupation. More recent mass strikes and factory takeovers in France and Italy bear striking similarities.

The idea of workers' councils represents more than a simple democratization of socialism. The evolution of the institution of self-management into the industrial basis of society sweeps aside the authoritarian forms and ideas that originally organized industrialization and transforms production into a free and conscious act. Self-management implies a transformation of human relations and represents an incipient set of values altogether different from the bourgeois, authoritarian values of the past. Because the goal of socialism in advanced industrial societies is not so much to increase the scale of production as to transform it, liberating values are at the core of the radical movement. For the same reason, an elitist or dictatorial party cannot represent those striving to accomplish this transformation. An elitist party can institute reforms, even substantial ones, but only those actively engaged in production can qualitatively alter their own social relations. Just as the Hungarian workers of 1956 acted for themselves through their workers' councils, so the movement for workers' control in France, Italy, and Britain stands outside the traditional authoritarian and centralist Left.

If the workers' control movement represents the most significant revival of libertarian socialism, Anarchist ideas are even more explicitly an aspect of the contemporary youth movement. The movement's values of community and individual liberty pose a social alternative to the totalitarianism of authoritarian and centrally directed industry. Liberated life-styles, the rejection of dominated and dominating social and sexual roles, communal living and problem-solving, community cooperatives and solidarity—all these tenets represent a vision of society and a "counter-society" clearly within the Anarchist tradition. The movement's emphasis on small groups, local autonomy, and its anti-leader bias are decidedly Anarchist in tone.

But rarely is the movement's natural Anarchism or intuitive understanding of liberty converted into a program of political action and organization. Instead, much of the Left still labors under a crude Leninist ideology and identifies revolution and the new society with the "Vanguard Party." Libertarian sentiments are abandoned to the barracks of new hierarchies and dogma, and, under this dominant definition of political action, anti-authoritarianism is restricted to a dream or to a life style, confined to the movement itself or to individuals. Anti-authoritarian action and agitation—by yippie types and others with neo-Anarchist tendencies—take on not the strengths but the historic weaknesses of the old Anarchism, the isolated protest and blind optimism of a movement with no program to transform real social relations. Anti-authoritarians in this situation may pose elements of the social problem, but they can offer no solutions, just as elitist parties may promise solutions but cannot identify the problem.

Aspects of the positive spirit of libertarian socialism are expressed in this description by Daniel and Gabriel Cohn-Bendit of the 22 March Movement, the group whose demonstrations triggered the mass strikes and uprisings of spring, 1968, in France:

> From the very start, the 22 March Movement made no distinction between leaders and led—all decisions were made in general assemblies and all reports by the various study commissions had to be referred back to it as well. This not only set a valuable example for the rank and file committees in the factories and the Action Committees in the streets but pointed the way to the future, showing how society can be run by all and for the benefit of all. In particular, the end of the division between leaders and led in our movement reflected the wish to abolish this division in the processes of production. Direct democracy implies direct management.[13]

This little collection outlines some of the chief issues and identifies some of the chief figures of the Anarchist movement. The collection is not a program; there are contradictions and gaps among the quotations, positions that the modern socialist movement would do well to emulate and others that it should make every effort to avoid. The only Anarchists included are socialists—more properly, either Anarchist Communists or Anarcho-syndicalists. I have included Proudhon, who did not advocate the complete abolition of private property, because he was essential to the birth of socialism and Anarchism; it is in any case but a short jump from Proudhon's "mutualism" to the full collectivism of Bakunin, a jump that most of his followers made. I have not included the Individualist Anarchists because they were not explicit socialists. Nor have I included the Christian Anarchism of Leo Tolstoy. Tolstoy was the theoretical founder of Anarchist pacifism, which has had a long and widespread impact. His movement was often characterized by its religious aspect, and he did not consider himself a part of the working-class socialist movement. Following his lead, I have left him out of the collection. As a result, there are no believers in God represented; neither are there any consistent principled pacifists. There were, of course, many Anarchist pacifists, but most of those who were not Tolstoyans can more properly be called anti-militarists; they believed that the revolution could be achieved peaceably through a general strike yet did not entirely rule out the possibility of violence.

The quotations are drawn from Anarchist pamphlets, polemics, memoirs, manifestos, and secondary sources, all from the Anarchist movements of Europe and North America. The date below each quotation is the earliest year connected with the writing—that is, the date of writing or the date of first publication. Doubtless, some of the dates should properly be earlier. I have altered translations here and there where the grammar or usage was confusing.

At the end of the book, there are biographical notes on some of the individuals and organizations quoted in these pages, which mention the best material currently available by or about them.

For their help and criticism, my thanks to my good friends Peggy Kaye, Michael Wallace, Edwin G. Burrows, Nunzio Pernicone, Stuart Gedal, Mark Naison, Francis Facciolo, and James P. Shenton.

NOTES

1. Michael Bakunin, "The Paris Commune and the Notion of the State." Quoted in Daniel Guerin, *Ni Dieu Ni Maître* (Paris, 1970).
2. Emma Goldman, *Anarchism and Other Essays* (New York, 1969).
3. *Statism and Anarchy.* Small sections of this work are published in English in Marshall Shatz, *The Essential Works of Anarchism* (New York, 1971).
4. *Anarcho-Syndicalism* (London, 1938), p. 76.
5. Quoted in *Selected Writings on Anarchism and Revolution,* edited by Martin Miller (Cambridge, Mass., 1970).
6. Gerald Brenan, *The Spanish Labyrinth* (Cambridge, England, 1964), pp. 180–81.
7. Franz Borkenau, *The Spanish Cockpit* (Ann Arbor, 1963), p. 71.
8. *Ceux de Barcelone* (Paris, 1937), pp. 217–26.
9. Noam Chomsky, *American Power and the New Mandarins* (New York, 1969). Collectivization statistics are cited from Communist sources in Stanley G. Payne, *The Spanish Revolution* (New York, 1970), chapter 11.
10. Cited in Burnett Bolloten, *The Grand Camouflage* (New York, 1961), p. 61.
11. Cited in Vernon Richards, *Lessons of the Spanish Revolution* (London, 1953).
12. Brenan, *op. cit.,* p. 325.
13. *Obsolete Communism; The Left-Wing Alternative* (London, 1969), p. 199.

WHAT IS ANARCHISM?

•

As man seeks justice in equality, so society seeks order in anarchy.

P.-J. PROUDHON, *What Is Property?* 1840

On our banner, the social-revolutionary banner, . . . are inscribed in fiery and bloody letters: the destruction of all States, the annihilation of bourgeois civilization, free and spontaneous organization from below upward, by means of free associations, the organization of the unbridled rabble of toilers, of all emancipated humanity, and the creation of a new universally human world.

MICHAEL BAKUNIN, *Statism and Anarchy*, 1873

"Anarchy" is Greek and means, verbatim, without ruler-ship; not being ruled. According to our vocabulary, anarchy is a state of society in which the only government is reason.

MICHAEL SCHWAB, courtroom speech after being sentenced to hang for Haymarket bombing (later commuted), 1886

Anarchism does not mean bloodshed; it does not mean robbery, arson, etc. These monstrosities are, on the contrary, the characteristic features of capitalism. Anarchism means peace and tranquillity to all. Anarchism, or socialism, means the reorganization of society upon scientific principles and the abolition of causes which produce vice and crime.

AUGUST SPIES, courtroom speech after being sentenced to hang for Haymarket bombing, 1886

What we want . . . is the complete destruction of the domination and exploitation of man by man; we want men united as brothers by a consensus and desired solidarity, all cooperating voluntarily for the well-being of all; we want society to be constituted for the purpose of supplying everybody with the means for achieving the maximum well-being, the maximum possible moral and spiritual development; we want bread, freedom, love and science—for everybody.

ERRICO MALATESTA, *Il Programma Anarchico,* 1920

Anarchism is the only philosophy which brings to man the consciousness of himself; which maintains that God, the State, and society are non-existent, that their promises are null and void, since they can be fulfilled only through man's subordination. Anarchism is therefore the teacher of the unity of life; not merely in nature, but in man. There is no conflict between the individual and the social instincts: the one the receptacle of a precious life essence, the other the repository of the element that keeps the essence pure and strong. The individual is the heart of society, conserving the essence of social life; society is the lungs which are distributing the element to keep the life essence—that is, the individual—pure and strong.

EMMA GOLDMAN, *Anarchism,* 1910

Anarchism was born of a moral revolt against social injustice. When men were found who felt suffocated by the social climate in which they were obliged to live; who felt the pain of others as if it were their own; who were also convinced that a large part of human suffering is not the inevitable consequence of inexorable natural or supernatural laws but, instead, stems from social realities dependent on human will and can be eliminated through human effort—the way was open that had to lead to anarchism.

The specific causes of social ills and the right means to destroy them had to be found. When some came to believe that the fundamental cause of the disease was the struggle between men which resulted in domination by the conquerors and the oppression and exploitation of the vanquished, when these men observed that domination by the former and the subjection of the latter had given rise to capitalistic property and the State, and when they sought to overthrow both State and property—then it was that anarchism was born.

ERRICO MALATESTA, *Pensiero e Volontà,* May 16, 1925

We do not fear, we invoke anarchy, convinced that this anarchy, that is to say, the complete manifestation of unchained popular life, must bring out liberty, equality, justice, the new order, and even the force of the Revolution against the reaction. This new life, the popular revolution, will without a doubt not wait to organize itself, but it will create its revolutionary organization from the bottom to the top and from the circumference to the center, conforming to the principle of liberty.

MICHAEL BAKUNIN, *Program and Object of the*
Secret Organization of
International Brothers, 1868

In a word, we reject all legislation, all authority, and all privileged, licensed, official, and legal influence, even though rising from universal suffrage, convinced that it can turn only to the advantage of a dominant minority of exploiters against the interests of the immense majority in subjection to them.

This is the sense in which we are really anarchists.

MICHAEL BAKUNIN, *God and the State,* 1871

Anarchy, today, is the attack, it is the war against all authority, against all power, against the State itself. In the future society, anarchy will be the defense, the obstacle used against the re-establishment of all authority, of all power, and of the State. Anarchy is the full and complete liberty of the individual who, freely and driven only by his needs, his tastes, and his sympathies, unites with other individuals in groups or in an association; the free development of associations which federate with other associations in the commune or in the neighborhood; the free development of the communes which federate together in the region—and thus would inevitably follow: the regions in the nation; the nations in humanity.

CARLO CAFIERO, *Anarchy and Communism,* 1880

In the fewest words, anarchism teaches that we can live in a society where there is no compulsion of any kind.

A life without compulsion naturally means liberty; it means freedom from being forced or coerced, a chance to lead the life that suits you best.

You cannot lead such a life unless you do away with the institutions that curtail your liberty and interfere with your life, the condition that compels you to act differently from the way you would like to.

ALEXANDER BERKMAN, *Now and After,* 1928

Of all social theories, Anarchism alone steadfastly proclaims that society exists for man, not man for society. The sole legitimate purpose of society is to serve the needs and advance the aspirations of the individual.

EMMA GOLDMAN, *The Place of the Individual
in Society,* 1930's

Anarchy is anti-government, anti-rulers, anti-dictators, anti-bosses and drivers. Anarchy is the negation of force; the elimination of all authority in social affairs; it is the denial of the right of domination of one man over another. It is the diffusion of rights, of power, of duties, equally and freely among the people.

ALBERT PARSONS, courtroom speech after being sentenced to hang for Haymarket bombing, 1886

It is not only against the abstract trinity of law, religion, and authority that we declare war. By becoming anarchists we declare war against all this wave of deceit, cunning, exploitation, depravity, vice—in a word, inequality—which they have poured into all our hearts. We declare war against their way of acting, against their way of thinking. The governed, the deceived, the exploited, the prostituted, wound above all else our sense of equality. It is in the name of equality that we are determined to have no more prostituted, exploited, deceived, and governed men and women.

PETER KROPOTKIN, *Anarchist Morality*, 1909

Anarchy and *communism*, far from howling at being found together, howl at not being found together, because these two terms, synonyms of *liberty* and *equality*, are the two necessary and indivisible terms of the revolution.

CARLO CAFIERO, *Anarchy and Communism*, 1880

Every anarchist is a socialist but every socialist is not necessarily an anarchist.

ADOLPH FISCHER, courtroom speech after being sentenced to hang for Haymarket bombing, 1886

When politics and home life have become one and the same thing, when economic problems have been solved in such a way that individual and collective interests are identical, then—all constraint having disappeared—it is evident that we will be in a state of total liberty or anarchy. Society's laws will operate by themselves through universal spontaneity, and they will not have to be ordered or controlled.

P.-J. PROUDHON, correspondence, 1864

You have hung in Chicago, decapitated in Germany, garroted in Jerez, shot in Barcelona, guillotined at Montbrison and at Paris, but you can never destroy anarchy. Its roots are too deep; it is born in the bosom of a rotten and disintegrating society; it is a violent reaction against the established order. It represents the egalitarian and libertarian aspirations which battle against present authority; it is everywhere, which makes it invisible. It will kill you in the end. That, gentlemen of the jury, is all I wish to say.

EMILE HENRY, courtroom speech, 1894

We contend for communism and anarchy—why? If we had kept silent, stones would have cried out. Murder was committed day by day. Children were slain, women worked to death, men killed inch by inch, and these crimes are never punished by law.

MICHAEL SCHWAB, on being sentenced to hang for Haymarket bombing, 1886

Anarchism does not mean plunder and outrage upon society; contrarily, its mission is to outroot the systematical plunder of a vast majority of the people by a comparatively few—the working classes by the capitalists. It aims at the extermination of the outrages committed by the reigning classes upon the wage-slaves under the name of "law and order."

ADOLPH FISCHER, on being sentenced to hang for Haymarket bombing, 1886

Anarchism asserts the possibility of an organization without discipline, fear, or punishment and without the pressure of poverty: a new social organism, which will make an end to the struggle for the means of existence—the savage struggle which undermines the finest qualities in man and ever widens the social abyss. In short, anarchism strives toward a social organization which will establish well-being for all.

EMMA GOLDMAN, *Living My Life,* 1931

Anarchism, then, really stands for the liberation of the human mind from the dominion of religion; the liberation of the human body from the dominion of property; liberation from the shackles and restraint of government. Anarchism stands for a social order based on the free groupings of individuals for the purpose of producing real social wealth; an order that will guarantee to every human being free access to the earth and full enjoyment of the necessities of life, according to individual desires, tastes, and inclinations.

Anarchism does not stand for military drill and uniformity; it does, however, stand for the spirit of revolt, in whatever form against everything that hinders human growth. All Anarchists agree in that, as they also agree in their opposition to the political machinery as a means of bringing about the great social change.

EMMA GOLDMAN, *Anarchism,* 1910

Anarchy—the absence of a master, of a sovereign—such is the form of government to which we are every day approximating, and which our accustomed habit of taking man for our measure and his will for law, leads us to regard as the height of disorder and the expression of chaos. The story is told that a citizen of Paris in the seventeenth century, having heard it said that in Venice there was no king, . . . could not recover from his astonishment and nearly died from laughter at the mere mention of so ridiculous a thing. So strong is our prejudice.

P.-J. PROUDHON, *What Is Property?* 1840

The idea of anarchism is the synthesis of liberalism and socialism, liberation of economics from the fetters of politics, liberation of culture from all political power, liberation of man by solidaric union with his kind.

RUDOLF ROCKER, *Nationalism and Culture,* 1933

No theory, no ready-made system, no book that has ever been written will ever save the world. I cleave to no system, I am a true seeker.

MICHAEL BAKUNIN, correspondence, n.d.

Beware of considering anarchy to be a dogma, a doctrine above question or debate, to be venerated by its adepts. . . . No! The absolute freedom which we demand constantly develops our thinking and raises it toward new horizons (according to the turn of mind of various individuals), takes it out of the narrow framework of regulation and codification. We are not "believers."

EMILE HENRY, note to his prison governor before being guillotined, 1894

One can be an anarchist irrespective of the philosophical system one prefers. There are materialist-anarchists as there are others, like myself, who without prejudicing future developments of the human mind, prefer simply to declare their ignorance in these matters.

Fortunately, philosophical concepts have little influence on conduct.

ERRICO MALATESTA, *Pensiero e Volontà,* July 1, 1925

We do not believe that we possess absolute truth; on the contrary, we believe that *social truth* is not a fixed quantity, good for all times, universally applicable, or determinable in advance, but that, instead, once freedom has been secured, mankind will go forward discovering and acting gradually with the least number of upheavals and with a minimum of friction. Thus our solutions always leave the door open to different and, one hopes, better solutions.

ERRICO MALATESTA, *Umanità Nova,*
September 16, 1921

Anarchism recognizes only the relative significance of ideas, institutions, and social forms. It is, therefore, not a fixed, self-enclosed social system but, rather, a definite trend in the historic development of mankind.

RUDOLF ROCKER, *Anarcho-Syndicalism,* 1938

Anarchism, at least as I understand it, leaves posterity free to develop its own particular systems, in harmony with its needs. Our most vivid imagination cannot foresee the potentialities of a race set free from external restraints. How, then, can anyone assume to map out a line of conduct for those to come? We, who pay dearly for every breath of pure, fresh air, must guard against the tendency to fetter the future. If we succeed in clearing the soil from the rubbish of the past and present, we will leave to posterity the greatest and safest heritage of all ages.

EMMA GOLDMAN, *Anarchism,* 1910

SMASH THE STATE

·

"THE INSTINCT TO COMMAND . . .
IS A . . . SAVAGE INSTINCT"

The instinct to command others, in its primitive essence, is a carnivorous, altogether bestial and savage instinct. Under the influence of the mental development of man, it takes on a somewhat more ideal form and becomes somewhat ennobled, presenting itself as the instrument of reason and the devoted servant of that abstraction, or political fiction, which is called the public good. But in its essence it remains just as baneful, and it becomes even more so when, with the application of science, it extends its scope and intensifies the power of its action. If there is a devil in history, it is this power principle.

MICHAEL BAKUNIN, *Protestation of the Alliance,* 1871

It is the characteristic of privilege and of every privileged position to kill the mind and heart of men. The privileged man, whether politically or economically, is a man depraved in mind and heart. That is a social law which admits of no exception and is as applicable to entire nations as to classes, corporations, and individuals.

MICHAEL BAKUNIN, *God and the State,* 1871

If there is an undeniable fact attested to a thousand times by experience, it is the corrupting effect of authority on those in whose hands it is placed.

The Jura Federation of the
First International, 1871

In the larger life of the society, the people are made to submit to the orders of those who were originally meant to serve them—the government and its agents. Once you do that, the power you have delegated will be used against you and your interests every time. And then you complain that your leaders "misuse their power." No, my friend, they don't misuse it; they only use it, for it is the *use* of power which is itself the worst misuse.

ALEXANDER BERKMAN, *What Is Communist
Anarchism?* 1928

Power operates only destructively, bent always on forcing every manifestation of life into the straitjacket of its laws. Its intellectual form of expression is dead dogma, its physical form brute force. And this unintelligence of its objectives sets its stamp on its supporters also and renders them stupid and brutal, even when they were originally endowed with the best of talents. One who is constantly striving to force everything into a mechanical order at last becomes a machine himself and loses all human feeling.

RUDOLF ROCKER, *Anarcho-Syndicalism,* 1938

I came to recognize that power, of whatever kind, must work out to be a curse. That is why I avow anarchism.

LOUISE MICHEL, speech on return to France
from exile, 1881

We understand that true liberty is not a matter of changing kings or rulers. We know that the whole system of master and slave must go, that the entire social scheme is wrong, that government and compulsion must be abolished, that the very foundations of authority and monopoly must be uprooted.

ALEXANDER BERKMAN, *What Is Communist Anarchism?* 1928

Straining for political power weakens the fibers of character and ideals. Daily contact with authority has strengthened my conviction that control of the governmental power is an illusory remedy for social ills. Inevitable consequences of false conceptions are not to be legislated out of existence. It is not merely the conditions but the fundamental ideas of present civilization that are to be transvalued, to give place to new social and individual relations.

ALEXANDER BERKMAN, letter from prison, 1905

Every power is animated by the wish to be the only power, because in the nature of its being it deems itself absolute and consequently opposes any bar which reminds it of the limits of its influence. Power is active consciousness of authority. Like God, it cannot endure any other God beside it.

RUDOLF ROCKER, *Nationalism and Culture,* 1933

It is the secret curse of every power that it becomes fatal, not only to its victims but to its possessors.

RUDOLF ROCKER, *Nationalism and Culture,* 1933

Every power presupposes some form of human slavery, for the division of society into higher and lower classes is one of the first conditions of its existence.

RUDOLF ROCKER, *Nationalism and Culture,* 1933

Between him who commands and him who obeys, and whose degradation deepens from generation to generation, there is no possibility of friendship.

ELISÉE RECLUS, *Mutual Good Will,* 1914

No one should be entrusted with power, inasmuch as anyone invested with authority must, through the force of an immutable social law, become an oppressor and exploiter of society.

MICHAEL BAKUNIN, *Statism and Anarchy,* 1873

The instinctive aims of those who govern—of those who frame the laws of the country as well as of those who exercise the executive power—are, because of their exceptional position, diametrically opposed to the instinctive popular aspirations. Whatever their democratic sentiments and intentions may be, viewing society from the high position in which they find themselves, they cannot consider this society in any other way but that in which a schoolmaster views his pupils. And there can be no equality between schoolmaster and pupils.

MICHAEL BAKUNIN, *The Bear of Berne and the Bear of St. Petersburg,* 1870

The strongest bulwark of authority is uniformity; the least divergence from it is the greatest crime.

EMMA GOLDMAN, *The Place of the Individual in Society,* 1930's

Does it follow that I reject all authority? Far from me, such a thought. In the matter of boots, I refer to the authority of the bootmaker; concerning houses, canals, or railroads, I consult that of the architect or engineer. For such and such knowledge I apply to such and such a specialist. But

I allow neither the bootmaker nor the architect nor the specialist to impose his authority on me. I listen to them freely and with all the respect merited . . . reserving always my incontestable right of criticism and censure.

MICHAEL BAKUNIN, *God and the State*, 1871

The dictator, the despot is always cowardly. He suspects treason everywhere. And the more terrified he becomes, the wilder rages his frightened imagination, incapable of distinguishing real danger from fancied. . . . Having chosen this course, the State is doomed to follow it to the very end.

ALEXANDER BERKMAN, *The Anti-Climax*, 1925

Nazism has been justly called an attack on civilization. This characterization applies with equal force to every form of dictatorship; indeed, to every kind of suppression and coercive authority. For what is civilization in the true sense? All progress has been essentially an enlargement of the liberties of the individual with a corresponding decrease of the authority wielded over him by external forces. This holds good in the realm of physical as well as of political and economic existence.

EMMA GOLDMAN, *The Place of the Individual
in Society*, 1930's

"GOVERNMENT . . . CORRUPTS EVERYTHING IT TOUCHES"

What must be abolished . . . to secure liberty?

First of all, of course, the thing that invades you most, that handicaps or prevents your free activity; the thing that interferes with your liberty and compels you to live differently from what would be your choice.

That thing is government.

Take a good look at it and you will see that government

is the greatest invader; more than that, the worst criminal man has ever known of. It fills the world with violence, with fraud and deceit, with oppression and misery. . . . It corrupts everything it touches.

ALEXANDER BERKMAN, *What Is Communist Anarchism?* 1928

Government is for slaves; free men govern themselves.

ALBERT PARSONS, on being sentenced to hang for Haymarket bombing, 1886

When we ask for the abolition of the State and its organs we are always told that we dream of a society composed of men better than they are in reality. But no, a thousand times, no. All we ask is that men should not be made worse than they are by such institutions!

PETER KROPOTKIN, *Anarchism, Its Philosophy and Ideal,* n.d.

Destruction of all political power is the first duty of the proletariat.

ERRICO MALATESTA, *Pensiero e Volontà,* July 1, 1926

If every Socialist will carry his thoughts back to an earlier date, he will no doubt remember the host of prejudices aroused in him when, for the first time, he came to the idea that abolishing the capitalist system and private appropriation of land and capital had become a historical necessity.

The same feelings are today produced in the man who for the first time hears that the abolition of the State, its laws, its entire system of management, governmentalism and centralization, also becomes a historical necessity: that the abolition of the one without the other is materially impossible. . . .

PETER KROPOTKIN, *Anarchism, Its Philosophy and Ideal,* n.d.

We no more accept the government of man by man than we accept the exploitation of man by man. . . .

P.-J. PROUDHON, *Confessions of a Revolutionary*, 1849

There must be no monarchy, no aristocracy, no democracy even, insofar as this implies a government acting in the name of the people and claiming to be the people. No authority, no government, even if it be popular government; this is the Revolution.

P.-J. PROUDHON, *The General Idea of the Revolution
in the Nineteenth Century*, 1851

Whether the government consists of one over the million, or a million over one, an anarchist is opposed to the rule of majorities as well as minorities.

ALBERT PARSONS, on being sentenced to hang, 1886

The more we are governed the less we are free.

ALBERT PARSONS, on being sentenced to hang, 1886

Human society marches forward; the State is always the brake.

The Workers' Federation of the District
of Courtelary, 1880

The abolition of the State is, we say, the task imposed upon the revolutionist—upon him, at least, who has the boldness of thought without which no revolution can be made. In this task he is opposed by all the traditions of the middle classes. But he has with him the whole evolution of humanity, which imposes upon us at the historic moment the job of freeing ourselves from a form of association perhaps made necessary by ignorance in times past but ultimately hostile to all further progress.

PETER KROPOTKIN, *Revolutionary Studies*, 1892

Only weak nations have strong governments.

CNT, *Solidaridad Obrera* (Barcelona), 1936

If a centralized power—government—is ruling the mass of the people (no matter whether this government "represents the will of the majority of the people" or not) it is enslaving them, and a direct violation of the laws of nature.

ADOLPH FISCHER, on being sentenced to hang, 1886

Yes: death—or renewal! *Either* the state forever, crushing individual and local life, taking over in all fields of human activity, bringing with it its wars and its domestic struggles for power, its palace revolutions which only replace one tyrant by another, and inevitably at the end of this development there is . . . death! *Or* the destruction of the state, and new life starting again in thousands of centers on the principle of the lively initiative of individual and groups and that of free agreement.

The choice lies with you!

PETER KROPOTKIN, *The State: Its Historic Role,* 1896

Why does everyone think that he can be decent enough without the policeman, but that the club is needed for "the others"?

ALEXANDER BERKMAN, *What Is Communist Anarchism?* 1928

We do not wish to be ruled. And by this very fact, do we not declare that we ourselves wish to rule nobody?

PETER KROPOTKIN, *Anarchist Morality,* 1909

The Character of Every State

Where the State begins, individual liberty ceases, and vice versa.

MICHAEL BAKUNIN, *Federalism, Socialism, and Anti-Theologism,* 1867

Ever since States came into existence, the political world has always been and still continues to be the stage for high knavery and unsurpassed brigandage—brigandage and knavery which are held in high honor, since they are ordained by patriotism, by transcendent morality, and by the supreme interest of the State. This explains to us why all the history of ancient and modern States is nothing more than a series of revolting crimes; why present and past kings and ministers of all times and all countries—statesman, diplomats, bureaucrats, and warriors—if judged from the point of view of simple morality and human justice, deserve a thousand times the gallows or penal servitude.

For there is no terror, cruelty, sacrilege, perjury, imposture, infamous transaction, cynical theft, brazen robbery, or foul treason which has not been and is not still being committed daily by representatives of the State, and with no other excuse, than this elastic, at times so convenient and terrible phrase *raison d'état*. A terrible phrase indeed! For it has corrupted and dishonored more people than Christianity itself. As soon as it is uttered, everything becomes silent and drops out of sight: honor, justice, right, pity itself vanishes, and with it logic and sound sense; black becomes white and white becomes black, the horrible becomes humane, and the most dastardly felonies and the most atrocious crimes become meritorious acts.

MICHAEL BAKUNIN, *Federalism, Socialism, and Anti-Theologism,* 1867

In politics, as in high finance, duplicity is regarded as a virtue.

MICHAEL BAKUNIN, *Statism and Anarchy,* 1873

It is . . . idle to talk of "Machiavellianism." What the Florentine statesman set forth so crisply and clearly and so unequivocably has always been practiced and will always be practiced as long as privileged minorities in society have the necessary power to subdue the great majority and to rob them of the fruits of their labor. Or is one to believe that our present secret diplomacy uses other principles?

RUDOLF ROCKER, *Nationalism and Culture*, 1933

Every type of political power presupposes some form of human slavery, for the maintenance of which it is called into being. Just as outwardly—that is, in relation to other States—the State has to create certain artificial antagonisms in order to justify its existence, so also internally the cleavage of society into castes, ranks, and classes is an essential condition of its continuance. The State is capable only of protecting old privileges and creating new ones; in that, its whole significance is exhausted.

RUDOLF ROCKER, *Anarcho-Syndicalism*, 1938

The State, then, is the most flagrant negation, the most cynical and complete negation of humanity. It rends apart the universal solidarity of all men upon earth, and it unites some of them only in order to destroy, conquer, and enslave all the rest. . . .

MICHAEL BAKUNIN, *Federalism, Socialism, and Anti-Theologism*, 1867

In all times and in all places, whatever be the name that the government takes, whatever has been its origin or its organization, its essential function is always that of oppressing and exploiting the masses, and of defending the oppressors and exploiters. Its principal characteristic and indispensable instruments are the policeman and the tax collector, the soldier and the prison. And to these are necessarily added the time-serving priest or the teacher. . . .

ERRICO MALATESTA, *Anarchy*, 1891

In the hands of the government everything becomes a means of exploitation, everything serves as a police measure, useful to hold the people in check. And it must be thus. If the life of mankind consists in strife between man and man, naturally there must be conquerors and conquered, and the government—which is the means of securing to the victors the results of their victory and perpetuating those results—will certainly never fall to those who have lost, whether the battle be on grounds of physical or intellectual strength, or in the field of economics.

ERRICO MALATESTA, *Anarchy*, 1891

All the political and civil organizations in the past and the present rest upon the following foundations: upon the historic fact of violence, upon the right to inherit property, upon the family rights of the father and the husband, and the conservation of all these foundations by religion. And all that taken together constitutes the essence of the State.

MICHAEL BAKUNIN, *Science and the Urgent Revolutionary Task*, 1870

The historic role of government is murder.

ALEXANDER BERKMAN, *Mother Earth*, November, 1912

The State denotes violence, oppression, exploitation, and injustice raised into a system and made into the cornerstone of the existence of any society. The State never had and never will have any morality. Its morality and only justice is the supreme interest of self-preservation and almighty power—an interest before which all humanity has to kneel in worship. The State is the complete negation of humanity, a double negation: the opposite of human freedom and justice, and the violent breach of the universal solidarity of the human race.

MICHAEL BAKUNIN, *Federalism, Socialism, and Anti-Theologism*, 1867

Governments oppress mankind in two ways—either directly, by brute force, that is, physical violence; or indirectly, by depriving them of the means of subsistence and thus reducing them to helplessness. Political power originated in the first method; economic privilege arose from the second. Governments can also oppress man by acting on his essential nature and in this way constitute religious authority.

ERRICO MALATESTA, *Anarchy,* 1891

In every State the government is nothing but a permanent conspiracy on the part of the minority against the majority, which it enslaves and fleeces. It follows clearly from the very essence of the State that there never has been and could not be a State organization that did not run counter to the interests of the people and that was not deeply hated by them.

MICHAEL BAKUNIN, *Science and the Urgent Revolutionary Task,* 1870

Every government has a twofold aim. One, the chief and avowed aim, consists in preserving and strengthening the State, civilization, and civil order—that is, the systematic and legalized dominance of the ruling class over the exploited people. The other aim is just as important in the eyes of the government, though less willingly avowed in the open, and that is the preservation of its exclusive governmental advantages and its personnel. The first aim is pertinent to the general interests of the ruling classes; the second, to the vanity and the exceptional advantages of the individuals in the government.

MICHAEL BAKUNIN, *Science and the Urgent Revolutionary Task,* 1870

No tyranny is more unendurable than that of an all-powerful bureaucracy which interferes with all the activities of men and leaves its stamp on them. . . . State capitalism, the most dangerous antithesis of real socialism, demands the surrender of all social activities to the state. It is the triumph of the machine over the spirit, the rationalization of all thought, action, and feeling according to the fixed norms of authority, and consequently the end of all intellectual culture.

RUDOLF ROCKER, *Nationalism and Culture*, 1933

Today, the State has succeeded in meddling in every aspect of our lives. From the cradle to the tomb, it strangles us in its arms. Sometimes as the central government, sometimes as the provincial or local State, now as the commune-State, it pursues us at each step, it appears at every street corner, it imposes on us, holds us, harasses us.

It regulates all our actions. It accumulates mountains of laws and ordinances in which the shrewdest lawyer is lost. Each day it creates new gears to awkwardly patch up the broken old watch, and it comes to create a machine so complex, so inferior, so obstructive, that it revolts even those who are charged with running it.

It creates an army of employees, spiders with hooked fingers, who know the universe only through the dirty windows of their offices, or by their obscure, absurd, illegible old papers, an evil band who have only one religion, that of the buck; only one care, that of hooking up with any party whatever in order to be guaranteed maximum political appointments for a minimum of work.

The results we know only too well.

PETER KROPOTKIN, *Words of a Rebel*, 1885

The State is an abstraction devouring the life of the people.

MICHAEL BAKUNIN, *Letters on Patriotism*, 1869

The State has no more existence than gods and devils have. They are equally the reflex and creation of man, for man, the *individual*, is the only reality. The State is but the shadow of man, the shadow of his opaqueness, of his ignorance and fear.

EMMA GOLDMAN, *The Place of the Individual in Society*, 1930's

The government—or the State, if you will—as judge, moderator of social strife, impartial administrator of the public interest, is a lie, an illusion, a Utopia, never realized and never realizable.

ERRICO MALATESTA, *Anarchy*, 1891

Whoever says political power says domination.

MICHAEL BAKUNIN, *The Bear of Berne and the Bear of St. Petersburg*, 1870

All political government must necessarily become despotic, because all government tends to become centralized in the hands of the few, who breed corruption among themselves and in a very short time disconnect themselves from the body of the people. The American republic is a good illustration.

LUCY PARSONS, interview with the New York *World*, 1886

The attitude of Anarcho-Syndicalism toward the political power of the present-day State is exactly the same as it takes toward the system of capitalist exploitation. Its adherents are perfectly clear that the social injustices of that system rest, not with its unavoidable excrescences, but in the capitalist economic order as such.

RUDOLF ROCKER, *Anarcho-Syndicalism*, 1938

I believe . . . that the state of castes and classes—the state where one class dominates and lives upon the labor of another class, and calls this order . . . is doomed to die and make room for a free society, voluntary association, or universal brotherhood, if you like. You may pronounce the sentence upon me, honorable judge, but let the world know that in A.D. 1886, in the State of Illinois, eight men were sentenced to death because they believed in a better future.

AUGUST SPIES, on being sentenced to hang, 1886

"Political Power and Wealth Are Inseparable"

The origins of government have been carefully studied and, all metaphysical conceptions as to its divine or "social contract" derivation having been laid aside, it appears that it is among us of a relatively modern origin, and that its powers have grown precisely in proportion as the division of society into the privileged and unprivileged classes was growing. . . .

PETER KROPOTKIN, *Anarchist Communism,* 1887

Are those who govern chosen from a certain class or party? Then, inevitably the ideas and interests of that class or party will triumph, and the wishes and interests of the others will be sacrificed.

ERRICO MALATESTA, *Anarchy,* 1891

Political power and wealth are inseparable. Those who have power have the means to gain wealth and must center all their efforts upon acquiring it, for without it they will not be able to retain their power. Those who are wealthy must become strong, for, lacking power, they run the risk of being deprived of their wealth. The toiling masses have always been powerless because they were poverty-stricken, and they were poverty-stricken because they lacked organized power.

MICHAEL BAKUNIN, *Science and the Urgent Revolutionary Task,* 1870

It follows that when government is abolished, wage slavery and capitalism must go with it, because they cannot exist without the support and protection of government.

ALEXANDER BERKMAN, *What Is Communist Anarchism?* 1928

The doctrinaire philosophers, as well as the jurists and economists, always assume that property came into existence before the rise of the State, whereas it is clear that the juridical idea of property, as well as family law, could arise historically only in the State, the first inevitable act of which was the establishment of this law of property.

MICHAEL BAKUNIN, *The Knouto-Germanic Empire,* 1871

Every exploitation of public economy by small minorities leads inevitably to political oppression, just as, on the other hand, every sort of political predominance must lead to the creation of new economic monopolies and hence to increased exploitation of the weakest sections of society. The two phenomena always go hand in hand. The will to power is always the will to exploitation of the weakest. . . .

RUDOLF ROCKER, *Nationalism and Culture,* 1933

Militarism

[It is] impossible to talk of Country and Patriotism without touching on that frightful wound of humanity: militarism.

JEAN GRAVE, *Dying Society and Anarchy,* 1893

War within and war without—such is the life of the government. It must be armed and ceaselessly on guard against both domestic and foreign enemies. Though itself breathing oppression and deceit, it is bound to regard all, within and outside its borders, as enemies, and must be in a state of conspiracy against all of them.

MICHAEL BAKUNIN, *Science and the Urgent Revolutionary Task,* 1870

Just as capitalist production and banking speculation—which in the long run swallows up that production—must, under the threat of bankruptcy, ceaselessly expand at the expense of the small financial and productive enterprises that they absorb, and become universal monopolistic enterprises extending all over the world—so this modern and necessarily military State is driven on by an irrepressible urge to become a universal State.

MICHAEL BAKUNIN, *Statism and Anarchy,* 1873

Every State, whether it is of a federative or a non-federative character, must strive, under the penalty of utter ruin, to become the most powerful of States. It has to devour others in order not to be devoured in turn.

MICHAEL BAKUNIN, *Federalism, Socialism, and Anti-Theologism,* 1867

Just as the State is always trying within its borders to abolish equality of social position among its subjects and to perpetuate this separation by differences of caste and class, so externally, too, it must take care to keep itself distinct from all other governmental organizations and to instill into its citizens the belief in their national superiority over all other peoples.

RUDOLF ROCKER, *Nationalism and Culture,* 1933

The modern State, by its essence and by the goals which it fixes, is necessarily a military State, and a military State is bound no less obligatorily to become a conquering State; if

it does not devote itself to conquest, it will itself be conquered, for the simple reason that everywhere force exists it
must be demonstrated. Hence, the modern State must necessarily be big and strong; that is the necessary condition of its
safety.

> MICHAEL BAKUNIN, *Statism and Anarchy,* 1873

The supreme law of the State is the augmentation of its
power to the detriment of internal liberty and external
justice.

> MICHAEL BAKUNIN, *The Bear of Berne and
> the Bear of St. Petersburg,* 1870

If you would remain men, be not soldiers; if you do not
know how to digest humiliations, do not put on the uniform.

> JEAN GRAVE, *Dying Society and Anarchy,* 1893

Law

Every great robbery that was ever perpetrated upon a
people has been by virtue of and in the name of law.

> ALBERT PARSONS, on being sentenced to hang, 1886

Like individual capital, which was born of fraud and
violence and developed under the auspices of authority, law
has no title to the respect of men. Born of violence and superstition, and established in the interests of consumer, priest,
and rich exploiter, it must be utterly destroyed on the day
when the people desire to break their chains.

> PETER KROPOTKIN, *Law and Authority,* 1886

The millions of laws which exist for the regulation of
humanity appear upon investigation to be divided into three
principal categories: protection of property, protection of

persons, protection of government. And by analyzing each of these three categories, we arrive at the same logical and necessary conclusion: *the uselessness and hurtfulness of law.*

PETER KROPOTKIN, *Law and Authority,* 1886

The first duty of the revolution will be to make a bonfire of all existing laws as well as of all titles to property.

PETER KROPOTKIN, *Law and Authority,* 1886

Whoever prescribes a rule of action for another to obey is a tyrant, usurper, and an enemy of liberty. This is precisely what every statute does. . . . In other words, a statute is the science of rascality, or the law of usurpation.

ALBERT PARSONS, on being sentenced to hang, 1886

It is not more laws which are required but less, and if we consider how existing laws operate on the people, and that there are upward of 400,000 laws in the statute book—enough to keep a man studying for the next few hundred years if he wished to become acquainted with them all—it is surely apparent to all that the law is impotent for good, and is only necessary because of the propertied interests behind it. . . . It has not changed its character one iota during a progress of centuries.

J. BLAIR SMITH, *Direct Action Versus Legislation,* 1899(?)

As all the laws about property, which make up thick volumes of codes and are the delight of our lawyers, have no other object than to protect the unjust appropriation of human labor by certain monopolists, there is no reason for their existence, and, on the day of the revolution, social revolutionists are thoroughly determined to put an end to them.

PETER KROPOTKIN, *Law and Authority,* 1886

A human law-maker, in my humble judgment, is a human humbug.

ALBERT PARSONS, on being sentenced to hang, 1886

The Ideology of the State

It was a great fallacy on the part of Jean-Jacques Rousseau to have assumed that primitive society was established by a free contract entered into by savages. But Rousseau was not the only one to uphold such views. . . .

A tacit contract! That is to say, a wordless and consequently thoughtless and will-less contract! A revolting nonsense! An absurd fiction, and what is more—a wicked fiction! An unworthy hoax! For it presupposes that while I was in the state of not being able to will, to think, to speak, I bound myself and my descendants—simply by reason of having let myself be victimized without raising any protest—into perpetual slavery.

The consequences of the *social contract* are in effect disastrous, for they lead to absolute domination by the State.

MICHAEL BAKUNIN, *Federalism, Socialism, and Anti-Theologism,* 1867

One might say . . . that inasmuch as the State is the product of a contract freely concluded by men, and since good is the product of the State, it follows that it is the product of liberty. This, however, would be an utterly wrong conclusion. The State, even according to this theory, is not the product of liberty, but on the contrary, the product of the voluntary negation and sacrifice of liberty.

MICHAEL BAKUNIN, *Federalism, Socialism, and Anti-Theologism,* 1867

Just as religion has fettered the human mind and as property, or the monopoly of things, has subdued and stifled man's needs, so has the State enslaved his spirit, dictating every phase of conduct. "All government in essence," says

Emerson, "is tyranny." It matters not whether it is government by divine right or by majority rule. In every instance its aim is the absolute subordination of the individual.

EMMA GOLDMAN, *Anarchism*, 1910

A common adoration, a common worship unites all the middle classes, all the exploiters. The chief of the State and the leader of the opposition, the pope and the bourgeois atheist, equally adore the same god, and this god of authority resides in the inmost recesses of their brain. This is why they remain united in spite of their differences.

PETER KROPOTKIN, *Revolutionary Studies*, 1892

The very existence of the State demands that there be some privileged class vitally interested in maintaining that existence. And it is precisely the group interests of that class that are called patriotism.

MICHAEL BAKUNIN, *Letters on Patriotism*, 1869

"The Best Form of Government . . . Is a Contradictory Idea"

The best form of government, like the most perfect religion, taken literally, is a contradictory idea. The problem is to discover how we can obtain, not the best government, but the greatest freedom. The only reality of power and politics is a liberty equal to, and identical with, order.

P.-J. PROUDHON, *Confessions of a Revolutionary*, 1849

History is there to teach us that all governments resemble one another and are worth the same. The best are the worst. More cynicism among some, more hypocrisy among others! At bottom, always the same proceedings, always the same intolerance! Government is liberal only in appearance, for it has in reserve, under the dust of legislative arsenals, some nice little law . . . for use against troublesome opposition.

Evil . . . in the eyes of the anarchists does not lie in

one form of government more than another. It is in the governmental idea itself, it is in the principle of authority.

PETER KROPOTKIN, courtroom speech in Lyons, 1883

General conclusion: *All political constitutions, from the most absolute monarchy to the reddest republic, offer an interest and guarantees only to the various privileged classes of the society. From the point of view of the people, they all equally represent the same exploitation and the same despotism.*

MICHAEL BAKUNIN, *The Political Theology of Mazzini,* fragment M, 1871

The State, every government, whatever its form, character, or color—be it absolute or constitutional, monarchy or republic, fascist, Nazi, or Bolshevik—is by its very nature conservative, static, intolerant of change and opposed to it. Whatever changes it undergoes are always the result of pressure exerted upon it, pressure strong enough to compel the ruling powers to submit, peaceably or otherwise, generally "otherwise"— that is, by revolution. Moreover, the inherent conservatism of government, of authority of any kind, unavoidably becomes reactionary.

EMMA GOLDMAN, *The Place of the Individual in Society,* 1930's

Every State, even the most republican and the most democratic State—even the would-be people's State conceived by Marx—is in its essence only a machine governing the masses from above, through an intelligent and therefore privileged minority, allegedly knowing the genuine interests of the people better than the people themselves.

MICHAEL BAKUNIN, *Statism and Anarchy,* 1873

There is not and there cannot be any good, just, or virtuous State. All States are bad, in this sense, that by their nature, by their basis, by all their conditions, and by the supreme end and aim of their existence they are completely the opposite of liberty, morality, and human justice.

> MICHAEL BAKUNIN, speech to the League of
> Peace and Freedom, 1867

In this matter of States, there are none virtuous but the powerless. And even they are criminal in their dreams.

> MICHAEL BAKUNIN, speech to the League of
> Peace and Freedom, 1867

The essential difference between a monarchy and a democratic republic is reduced to the following: In a monarchy, the bureaucratic world oppresses and plunders the people for the greater benefit of the privileged propertied classes as well as for its own benefit, and all that is done in the name of the monarch; in a republic, the same bureaucracy does exactly the same thing, but in the name of the will of the people.

> MICHAEL BAKUNIN, *Statism and Anarchy*, 1873

Tyranny and crime are equally deserving of condemnation no matter whether they exist under the red-yellow flag of the Monarchy or the tricolor of the Republic or even under the red banner of the Dictatorship of the Proletariat.

> CNT, *Solidaridad Obrera* (Barcelona), 1935

In an absolutism, the autocrat is visible and tangible. The real despotism of republican institutions is far deeper, more insidious, because it rests on the popular delusion of self-government and independence. That is the source of democratic tyranny.

> ALEXANDER BERKMAN, letter from prison, 1901

The bourgeoisie in all the countries of Europe most of all fears the social revolution; it knows that against this storm it has no other refuge but the State. That is why it always desires and demands *a strong State,* or, in plain language, a military dictatorship. And in order to bamboozle the masses of the people more easily, it aims to invest this dictatorship with the forms of a popular representative government, which would allow it to exploit the great masses of the people *in the very name of the people.*

MICHAEL BAKUNIN, *Statism and Anarchy,* 1873

Experience shows in effect that everywhere and at all times the government—however popular it may have been at its origin—is ranged on the side of the most enlightened and richest class against the poorest and the most numerous one; that after proving a few times that it is liberal, it becomes little by little exceptional, exclusive; finally, that, instead of sustaining liberty and equality among all, it works obstinately to destroy them, by virtue of its natural inclination to privilege.

P.-J. PROUDHON, *The General Idea of the Revolution in the Nineteenth Century,* 1851

Monarchical absolutism is unspeakably clumsy, stupidly exposing itself to rebellion and uprisings. But the ballot box is the most potent factor for well-ordered oppression and exploitation. It hypnotizes its victims into the belief of political sovereignty and independence, while at the same time still firmer riveting the chains of bondage.

EMMA GOLDMAN, *Mother Earth,* October, 1910

Universal suffrage is the counterrevolution.

P.-J. PROUDHON, revolutionary propaganda, 1848

It is clear to me that universal suffrage is the most extensive and at the same time the most refined manifestation of the political charlatanism of the State; a dangerous instrument without doubt, and demanding a great deal of skill and competence of those who make use of it, but becoming at the same time—that is, if those people learn to make use of it—the surest means of making the masses cooperate in the construction of their own prison.

MICHAEL BAKUNIN, *The Knouto-Germanic Empire,* 1871

Universal suffrage is a powerful means of putting human activity to sleep. It has nothing in common with popular sovereignty, except the right to be at all times sovereign over others. It has nothing in common with equality.

PARAF-JAVAL, *Free Examination,* 1903

The voter is a man who comes where he is summoned one day like a flunkey, to one who whistles for him as for a dog trained to obey, who comes on the said day only and not on any other day. He is a man who comes when authority says: "The moment is here to sanction one more time a system established by others and for others than yourself. The moment is here to choose those who will be part of this system with or without the intention of modifying it; to choose those who, for contributing to the functioning of the machine that crushes the weak, will be paid in silver, in influence, in privileges, in honors. The moment is here to put aside one more time the idea of revolt against the organization that exploits you and to obey its authority. The moment is here to vote, that is to say, to make an act which signifies: I RECOGNIZE YOUR LAWS."

Is it not clear that the first meaning of abstaining from elections is this: "I DO NOT RECOGNIZE THE LAWS"?

It follows that any voter (whether justly called monarchist, or wrongly socialist-revolutionary) is a conservative, since the result of his vote is to contribute to making the system function with vigor.

PARAF-JAVAL, *The Absurdity of Politics,* 1904

Under universal suffrage the elected are those who know best how to take in the masses.

ERRICO MALATESTA, *Anarchy,* 1891

Universal suffrage is a means of stifling that individual initiative which we proclaim, and which we must, quite to the contrary, seek to develop with all our strength. Universal suffrage is an instrument of authority while we pursue the complete liberation of human individuality; it is an instrument of repression while we seek to inspire revolt. Far from being able to serve us, universal suffrage can only shackle us; we must combat it.

JEAN GRAVE, *Dying Society and Anarchy,* 1893

Ye fools! who dream that statecraft can do aught
But limit freedom to the beaten track,
Where economic slaves their daily task
Perform, and when ye rise relief to ask
Do find your ballots have for others wrought
And clothed with power to drive you trembling back.

DYER D. LUM, *Revolutionary Almanack,* 1914

This is the vote: the hide of a sonorous ass, which gives sounds only under the blows of those who want to make it speak.

JEAN GRAVE, *Dying Society and Anarchy,* 1893

America is just the country that shows how all the written guarantees in the world for freedom are no protection against tyranny and oppression of the worst kind. There the politician has come to be looked upon as the very scum of society.

PETER KROPOTKIN, speech in London, 1891

The poor, stupid, free American citizen! Free to starve, free to tramp the highways of this great country, he enjoys universal suffrage, and, by that right, he has forged chains about his limbs.

EMMA GOLDMAN, *Woman Suffrage,* 1910

To preclude errors, it would be advisable to amend the [U.S.] Constitution in such a manner as to make it quite clear that free speech is permitted only to ex-Presidents, manufacturers' associations, politicians, and priests.

ALEXANDER BERKMAN, *Mother Earth,* June, 1911

Political rights do not exist because they have been legally set down on a piece of paper, but only when they have become the ingrown habits of a people, and when any attempt to impair them will meet with the violent resistance of the populace. Where this is not the case, there is no help in any parliamentary opposition or any Platonic appeals to the constitution.

RUDOLF ROCKER, *Anarcho-Syndicalism,* 1938

The point of attack in the political struggle lies, not in the legislative bodies, but in the people. Political rights do not originate in parliaments; they are, rather, forced upon parliaments from without. And even their enactment into law has for a long time been no guarantee of their security. . . . Governments . . . are always inclined to restrict or to abrogate completely rights and freedoms that have been achieved if they imagine that the people will put up no resistance.

RUDOLF ROCKER, *Anarcho-Syndicalism,* 1938

Our studies of the preparatory stages of all revolutions bring us to the conclusion that not a single revolution has originated in parliaments or in any other representative assembly. *All began with the people.*

PETER KROPOTKIN, *Modern Science and Anarchism,* 1913

Neither heredity, nor election, nor universal suffrage, nor the excellence of the sovereign, nor the consecration of religion and of time can make royalty legitimate. Whatever form it takes—monarchic, oligarchic, or democratic—royalty, or the government of man by man, is illegitimate and absurd.

P.-J. PROUDHON, *What Is Property?* 1840

"REVOLUTION AND GOVERNMENT ARE INCOMPATIBLE"

We know that revolution and government are incompatible. One must destroy the other no matter what name is given to government, whether dictatorship, royalty, or parliament. We know that what makes the strength and the truth of our party is contained in this formula—"Nothing good or durable can be done except by the free initiative of the people, and every government tends to destroy it." And so the very best among us, if they should become masters of that formidable machine, the government, would become in a week fit only for the gallows if their ideas had not to pass through the crucible of the popular mind before being put into execution.

PETER KROPOTKIN, *Revolutionary Government,* 1892

The political State, whatever its form, and constructive revolutionary effort are irreconcilable. They are mutually exclusive. Every revolution in the course of its development faces this alternative: to build freely, independently, and despite the government, or to choose government, with all the limitation and stagnation it involves. The path of the Social Revolution, of the constructive self-reliance of the organized, conscious masses, is in the direction of non-government; that is, of Anarchy.

ALEXANDER BERKMAN, *The Anti-Climax,* 1925

Absolute monarchy corresponds to the system of serfdom. Representative government corresponds to capital-rule. Both, however, are class-rule. But in a society where the distinction between capitalist and laborer has disappeared, there is no need for such a government; it would be an anachronism, a nuisance. Free workers would require a free organization, and this cannot have any other basis than free agreement and free cooperation, without sacrificing the autonomy of the individual to the all-pervading interference of the State. The no-capitalist system implies the no-government system.

PETER KROPOTKIN, *Anarchist Communism,* 1887

No authority, no government, even if it be popular government; this is the revolution.

P.-J. PROUDHON, *The General Idea of Revolution in the Nineteenth Century,* 1851

It is a contradiction in terms to say that a government can be revolutionary, for the simple reason that it is the government. Only society—that is, the masses inspired with intelligence—can revolutionize itself, because only society can make rational use of its own spontaneous energy, can analyze and explain the mystery of its destiny and origins, can change its faith and its philosophy—and, finally, because only society is capable of struggling against its creator and producing its own fruit.

P.-J. PROUDHON, *Confessions of a Revolutionary,* 1849

Just as the functions of the bodily organs of plants and animals cannot be arbitrarily altered, so that, for example, one cannot at will hear with his eyes and see with his ears, so also one cannot at pleasure transform an organ of social repression into an instrument for the liberation of the oppressed. The state can only be what it is: the defender of mass exploitation and social privileges, the creator of privileged classes and castes and of new monopolies.

RUDOLF ROCKER, *Anarcho-Syndicalism,* 1938

If tomorrow there should be established a government or a legislative council, a parliament made up exclusively of workers, those very workers who are now staunch democrats and socialists will become determined aristocrats, bold or timid worshippers of the principle of authority, and will also become oppressors and exploiters.

MICHAEL BAKUNIN, *The Bear of Berne and the Bear of St. Petersburg,* 1870

I am *the absolute enemy of a revolution by decrees,* which is . . . *a reaction disguised by revolutionary appearances.* As against the system of revolutionary decrees, *I oppose the system of revolutionary action,* the only effective, consistent, and true system. The authoritarian system of decrees, in seeking to *impose* freedom and equality, destroys them. *The Anarchist system of action evokes and creates them in an infallible manner,* without the intervention of any official or authoritarian violence whatever.

MICHAEL BAKUNIN, *Letters to a Frenchman,* 1870

Dictatorship is the negation of organic development, of natural building from below upward; it is the proclamation of wardship over the toiling people, a guardianship forced upon the masses by a tiny minority. *Even if its supporters are animated by the very best intentions,* the iron logic of the facts will always drive them into the camp of extremist despotism. . . . Such a thing as the dictatorship of class is utterly unthinkable, since it will always involve merely the dictatorship of a particular party, which takes it upon itself to speak *in the name of a class,* just as the bourgeoisie justified any despotic proceeding *in the name of the people.*

RUDOLF ROCKER, *Anarcho-Syndicalism,* 1938

[A] bloody revolution founded on the construction of a powerfully centralized revolutionary State would have as its inevitable result . . . the military dictatorship of a new master. The triumph of the Jacobins . . . would thus be the death of the Revolution.

We are the natural enemies of these revolutionaries, future dictators, regulators, and tutors of the revolution, who, before the monarchist, aristocratic, and bourgeois States of the present have even been destroyed, already dream of the creation of new revolutionary States, as centralized and more despotic than the States that exist today.

MICHAEL BAKUNIN, *Program and Object of the Secret Revolutionary Organization of International Brothers,* 1868

If some people will have assumed the right to violate anybody's freedom on the pretext of preparing the triumph of freedom, they will always find that the people are not yet sufficiently mature, that the dangers of reaction are ever-present, that the education of the people has not yet been completed. And with these excuses they will seek to perpetuate their own power—which could begin as the strength of a people up in arms, but which, if not controlled by a profound feeling for the freedom of all, would soon become a real government, no different from the governments of today.

ERRICO MALATESTA, *La Questione Sociale,* November 25, 1899

What do we understand by revolution? It is not a simple change of governors. It is the taking possession by the people of all social wealth. It is the abolition of all the forces that have so long hampered the development of humanity. . . . In order that the taking possession of social wealth should become an accomplished fact, it is necessary that the people should have their hands free, that they should shake off the slavery to which they are too much habituated, that they act according to their own will and march forward without waiting for orders from anyone. And it is this very thing that a dictatorship would prevent, however well intentioned it might be, while it would be incapable of advancing in the slightest degree the march of the revolution.

PETER KROPOTKIN, *Revolutionary Government,* 1881

The fact of expropriation must be accomplished by the workers of the towns and countryside themselves. To hope that any government whatever would do it would be a profound error: for history teaches us that governments, even those that come from the revolution, never do anything but give legal sanction to the accomplished facts of the revolution, and even then, the people must undertake a long struggle with these governments to force them to assent to the revolutionary measures that they used to loudly proclaim during the period of effervescence. Besides, a measure as important as expropriation would remain a dead letter unless it were freely realized in each commune, in each place of the territory, by the interested persons themselves.

PETER KROPOTKIN, report to the
Jura Federation, 1879

It is necessary to remark—and this is directed, above all, to our adversaries, the authoritarian and statist communists— that the taking possession and the enjoyment of all of the existing wealth must be . . . done by the people themselves. . . . No intermediaries, no representatives who always, in the end, represent only themselves, no moderators of equality, no more moderators of liberty, no new government, no new State, whether it be called people's or democratic, revolutionary or provisional!

CARLO CAFIERO, *Anarchy and Communism,* 1880

Socialism without Anarchy—that is, state socialism—seems impossible to us, since it would be destroyed by the very organism destined to support it. Anarchy without socialism seems equally impossible to us.

ERRICO MALATESTA, *l'Anarchia,* August, 1896

Socialism . . . —whatever form it may take in its evolution toward communism—must find *its own form* of political organization. . . . Socialism *cannot* utilize representative government as a weapon for liberating labor, just as it cannot utilize the church and its theory of divine right, or imperialism and Caesarism, with its theory of hierarchy of functionaries, for the same purpose.

A new form of political organization has to be worked out the moment socialist principles enter our life. And it is evident that this new form will have to be *more popular, more decentralized, and nearer to the folkmoot self-government* than representative government can ever be.

PETER KROPOTKIN, *Modern Science and Anarchism,* 1913

To defend, to save the revolution, there is only one means: that of pushing the revolution as far as it will go.

ERRICO MALATESTA, *Fede!,* November 25, 1923

The revolution is a thing of the people, a popular creation; the counterrevolution is a thing of the State. It has always been so, and will always be so, whether in Russia, Spain, or China.

Anarchist Federation of Iberia (FAI), *Tierra y Libertad,* July 3, 1936

The differences between a revolutionary dictatorship and a State are merely external. In essence they both represent government of the majority by a minority in the name of the alleged stupidity of the former and the alleged intelligence of the latter. Therefore they are both equally reactionary, both of them having the direct and unavoidable result of consolidating the political and economic privileges of the ruling minority and the political and economic slavery of the masses.

MICHAEL BAKUNIN, *Statism and Anarchy,* 1873

Karl Marx and His Followers

We ignore neither the genius not the power of Karl Marx's work, but we consider that his authoritarian conception of socialism has poisoned the proletarian movement.

Marxism tends to make the workers not free men, but resigned.

Today, as yesterday, against the authoritarian and Statist socialist conceptions of Karl Marx, we support the libertarian and federalist socialist conceptions of Michael Bakunin.

JEAN GRAVE, *The Society of Nations*, 1918

According to the almost unanimous opinion of the German socialists, *a political revolution has to precede a social revolution*—which, in my opinion, is a grave error, because every *political revolution* that takes place prior to and consequently apart from a social revolution necessarily will be a bourgeois revolution, and a bourgeois revolution can only further bourgeois socialism; that is, it will necessarily end in new exploitation of the proletariat by the bourgeoisie—exploitation perhaps more skillful and hypocritical, but certainly no less oppressive.

MICHAEL BAKUNIN, *Letters to a Frenchman*, 1870

The Marxists claim that only a dictatorship, well understood to be their own, can create popular liberty; to this we respond that no dictatorship can have any goal but to last as long as possible, and that it is capable only of engendering slavery in the people who submit to it and of educating them to that slavery; liberty can be created only by liberty—that is to say, by the uprising of the entire people and by the free organization of the working masses from the bottom up.

MICHAEL BAKUNIN, *Statism and Anarchy*, 1873

Behind all the democratic and socialistic phrases and promises of Marx's program, there is to be found in his

State everything that constitutes the true despotic and brutal nature of all States, whatever the form of their government.

MICHAEL BAKUNIN, fragment continuation of
The Knouto-Germanic Empire, 1872

[Marx] says, "Poverty produces political slavery, the State," but he does not allow this to be turned around to say, "Political slavery, the State, reproduces in its turn, and maintains, poverty as the condition of its own existence; so that, in order to destroy poverty, it is necessary to destroy the State!"

MICHAEL BAKUNIN, letter to *La Liberté,* October, 1872

According to the theory of Marx, the people not only must not destroy [the State] but must strengthen it and put it at the complete disposal of their benefactors, guardians, and teachers—the leaders of the Communist Party, namely Mr. Marx and his friends—who will proceed to liberate [mankind] in their own way. They will hold the reins of government in a strong hand, because the ignorant people require an exceedingly firm guardianship; they will establish a single state bank, concentrating in its hands all commercial, industrial, agricultural, and even scientific production, and then will divide the masses into two armies—industrial and agricultural—under the direct command of the state engineers, who will constitute a new privileged scientific-political estate.

MICHAEL BAKUNIN, *Statism and Anarchy,* 1873

It is time to have done will all popes and priests; we want them no longer, even if they call themselves Social Democrats.

MICHAEL BAKUNIN, *God and the State,* 1871

Dictatorship of the proletariat signifies the dictatorship of all—that is to say, that which would not be a dictatorship, as a government of all is not a government in the authoritarian, historical, and practical sense of the word.

But the true partisans of the "dictatorship of the proletariat" do not understand it thus, and they are doing well indeed in Russia.

ERRICO MALATESTA, letter to Luigi Fabbri, July, 1919

One may ask, then, if the proletariat is to be the ruling class, over whom will it rule? The answer is that there will remain another proletariat which will be subjected to this new domination, this new State. It may be, for example, the peasant "rabble," which, as we know, does not stand in great favor with the Marxists.

MICHAEL BAKUNIN, *Statism and Anarchy,* 1873

The [Marxists] imagine that they can achieve it [the emancipation of mankind] by the development and organization of the political power of the working classes, and particularly of the town proletariat. . . . The revolutionary socialists . . . think, on the other hand, that they can reach this goal only by the development and organization of the nonpolitical, social, and therefore antipolitical power of the working masses in town and country.

MICHAEL BAKUNIN, polemic against Marx, 1872(?)

A universal state, government, dictatorship! The dream of Popes Gregory VII and Boniface VIII, of the Emperor Charles V, and of Napoleon, reproducing itself under new forms, but always with the same pretensions in the camp of Socialist Democracy! Can one imagine anything more burlesque, but also anything more revolting?

To maintain that one group of individuals, even the most intelligent and the best intentioned, is capable of becoming the thought, the soul, the guiding and unifying will of the revolutionary movement and of the economic organization of the proletariat in all countries is such a heresy against common sense, and against the experience of history, that one asks with astonishment how a man as intelligent as Marx could have conceived it.

MICHAEL BAKUNIN, letter to *La Liberté*, October, 1872

According to them [the Marxists], the yoke of the State, this dictatorship, is a necessary phase of transition to arrive at the total emancipation of all the people: anarchy or liberty being the goal, the State or dictatorship the means. Thus, then, in order to emancipate the masses of the people, one must begin by enslaving them.

MICHAEL BAKUNIN, *Statism and Anarchy*, 1873

I think that Marx is a very serious revolutionary, if not always very sincere, and that he really wants the uprising of the masses; and I ask myself how he could ever fail to see that the establishment of a universal dictatorship, collective or individual, a dictatorship that would in some ways necessitate an engineer-in-chief of the world revolution, ruling and directing the insurrectional movement of the masses in all countries as one runs a machine—that the establishment of such a dictatorship would itself suffice to kill the revolution, to paralyse and warp all the great popular movements?

MICHAEL BAKUNIN, letter to *La Liberté*, October, 1872

Between the Marxian policy and the Bismarckian policy, there is no doubt a very appreciable difference, but between the Marxists and ourselves, there is an abyss. They are Governmentalists, we are out and out Anarchists.

MICHAEL BAKUNIN, letter to *La Liberté*, October, 1872

We too aspire to communism as the most perfect achievement of human solidarity, but it must be anarchist communism—that is, freely desired and accepted, and the means by which the freedom of everyone is guaranteed and can expand; for these reasons we maintain that State communism, which is authoritarian and imposed, is the most hateful tyranny that has ever afflicted, tormented, and handicapped mankind.

ERRICO MALATESTA, *Umanità Nova,* August 31, 1921

However much we detest the democratic lie, which in the name of the "people" oppresses the people in the interests of a class, we detest even more, if that is possible, the dictatorship which, in the name of the "proletariat," places all the strength and the very lives of the workers in the hands of the creatures of a so-called Communist party, who perpetuate their power and in the end reconstruct the capitalist system for their own advantage.

ERRICO MALATESTA, *Umanità Nova,* August 31, 1921

In the People's State of Marx, there will be, we are told, no privileged class at all. All will be equal, not only from the juridical and political point of view, but from the economic point of view. . . . There will therefore be no longer any privileged class, but there will be a government and, note this well, an extremely complex government, which will not be content with governing and administering the masses politically, as all governments do today, but will also administer them economically, concentrating in its own hands the production and just division of wealth. . . . It will be the reign of *scientific intelligence,* the most aristocratic, despotic, arrogant, and contemptuous of all regimes. There will be a new class, a new hierarchy of real and pretended scientists and scholars, and the world will be divided into a minority ruling in the name of knowledge and an immense majority. And then, woe betide the mass of ignorant ones!

MICHAEL BAKUNIN, fragment continuation of
The Knouto-Germanic Empire, 1872

Every State, whether bourgeois or socialist, is but a gendarme either guarding the capitalist order, under the domination of the bourgeois, or the state order under socialism. The State always stands on guard in the interests of the bosses. This is its function, the one reason for its existence.

The Soviet State differs from other states by combining the functions of both the gendarme and the boss. It begot a new class, the present ruling class, which exercises the power of dictatorship. . . . The Socialist State cannot abolish classes. It does away with old classes, the bourgeois and proletariat, replacing them with new ones. Lords and those who are lorded over, rulers and ruled, masters and slaves.

> Foreign Bureau to Promote an All-Russian
> Anarcho-Syndicalist Convention, 1922

If the world could be set free by decrees, there would long ago have been no problems in Russia.

> RUDOLF ROCKER, *Anarcho-Syndicalism*, 1938

One thing is indisputable. Even if the dictatorship of the party were an appropriate means to bring about a blow to the capitalist system (which I strongly doubt), *it is nevertheless harmful for the creation of a new socialist system.* What are necessary and needed are local institutions, local forces; but there are none, anywhere. Instead of this, wherever one turns there are people who have never known anything of real life, who are committing the gravest errors which have been paid for with thousands of lives and the ravaging of entire districts.

> PETER KROPOTKIN, letter to Lenin, 1920

Only by suppressing each government, each representative of authority, by destroying at the base each political, economic, and statist lie, by destroying the State through a social revolution, will we be able to realize a true system of soviets of workers and peasants and to advance toward socialism.

> Program-Manifesto of the Makhnovitsi (revolutionary partisan army of the Ukraine), 1920

General Bonaparte defended the French Revolutions against the European reaction, but in defending it, he strangled it. Lenin, Trotsky, and their comrades are surely sincere revolutionaries . . . and they will not be traitors; but they are preparing the governmental cadres that will serve those who will come later to profit from the revolution and to assassinate it. They themselves will be the first victims of their methods, and I fear that the revolution will crumble along with them.

> ERRICO MALATESTA, letter to Luigi Fabbri, July, 1919

We are learning to know in Russia how *not* to introduce communism, even with a people tired of the old regime and opposing no active resistance to the experiments of the new rulers. . . .

> PETER KROPOTKIN, letter to the workers of Western Europe, 1919

It is not so much the Bolsheviki who killed the Russian Revolution as the Bolshevik idea. It was Marxism, however modified; in short, fanatical governmentalism.

> EMMA GOLDMAN, *My Disillusionment in Russia,* 1922

It is a question of crushing fascism once and for all. Yes, and in spite of government.

No government in the world fights fascism to the death. When the bourgeoisie sees power slipping from its grasp, it has recourse to fascism to maintain itself. . . .

We know what we want. To us it means nothing that there

is a Soviet Union somewhere in the world, for the sake of whose peace and tranquility the workers of Germany and China were sacrificed to fascist barbarians by Stalin. We want the revolution here in Spain, right now, not maybe after the next European war. . . .

I do not expect any help for a libertarian revolution from any government in the world.

BUENAVENTURA DURRUTI, from an interview during the Spanish Civil War, 1936

There is in this program [of Messers. Marx and Engels] another expression that is profoundly repugnant to us revolutionary anarchists, who frankly want the complete emancipation of the people: it is the proletariat, the world of workers, presented as a *class*, not as a *mass*. Do you know what this means? Neither more nor less than a new aristocracy, that of factory and town workers, to the exclusion of the millions who constitute the proletariat of the countryside and who, in the forecasts of Messers. Social Democrats of Germany, will become the proper subjects of the great so-called People's State.

MICHAEL BAKUNIN, letter to *La Liberté,* October, 1872

The Marxists do not reject our program absolutely. They only reproach us with wanting to hasten, to outstrip the slow march of history, and to ignore the scientific law of successive evolution. Having had the thoroughly German nerve to proclaim in their works, devoted to the philosophical analysis of the past, that the bloody defeat of the insurgent peasants of Germany and the triumph of the despotic states in the sixteenth century constituted great revolutionary progress, they today have the nerve to satisfy themselves with establishing a new despotism, to the so-called profit of the urban workers and to the detriment of the toilers in the country.

MICHAEL BAKUNIN, letter to *La Liberté,* October, 1872

It seems unbelievable that even today, after everything that has happened and is happening in Russia, there are people who still imagine that the difference between socialists and anarchists is only that of wanting revolution gradually or quickly.

ERRICO MALATESTA, *Umanità Nova,* September 3, 1921

Marx is not only a learned Socialist, he is also a very clever politician and an ardent patriot.

MICHAEL BAKUNIN, fragment continuation of
The Knouto-Germanic Empire, 1872

Karl Marx is a man of immense statistical and economic knowledge. His work on capital, though unfortunately bristling with formulas and metaphysical subtleties, which render it unapproachable for the great mass of readers, is in the highest degree a scientific or realist work: in the sense that it absolutely excludes any other logic than that of the facts.

MICHAEL BAKUNIN, polemic against Marx, 1872(?)

We have heard much of late about the "dialectical method," which was recommended for formulating the socialist ideal. Such a method we do not recognize; nor do the modern natural sciences have anything to do with it.

PETER KROPOTKIN, *Modern Science and
Anarchism,* 1913

"CAPITALISM IS THE GREATEST CRIME OF ALL"

Capitalism is the greatest crime of all; . . . it devours more lives in a single day than all the murderers put together.

ALEXANDER BERKMAN, *What Is Communist Anarchism?* 1928

If I had to answer the question "What is slavery?" and if I were to answer in one word, "Murder," I would immediately be understood. I would not need to use a lengthy argument to demonstrate that the power to deprive a man of his thoughts, his will, and his personality is a power of life and death, and that to enslave a man is to murder him. Why, then, to the question "What is property?" may I not likewise reply "theft" without knowing that I am certain to be misunderstood, even though the second proposition is simply a transformation of the first?

P.-J. PROUDHON, *What Is Property?* 1840

It is clear . . . that if it is desirable that a person beginning to work not enslave himself, not yield part of his labor, his strength, his independence, either permanently or temporarily, to private individuals whose arbitrariness always will determine how great that part should be, then it is necessary that private persons control neither the instruments of labor (tools, machines, factories), nor the places of cultivation of the raw products (the earth), nor the raw products stored up beforehand, nor the means for storing up and conveying them to a given place . . . nor the means of existence during work (the supplies of the means of subsistence and housing).

Thus we arrive at the elimination, in that future system whose realization we desire, of any personal property, of any property of an associated joint stock company, a cartel, and so forth.

PETER KROPOTKIN, *Must We Occupy Ourselves . . . ?* 1873

We require the abolition of this . . . wage system. We call upon all men to refuse to pay for anything. We know that this course will make it impossible to receive pay for anything.

The Chicago *Alarm,* newspaper of the International Working People's Association, 1886

The abolition of individual property, in the literal sense of the word, will come, if it comes, by the force of circumstances, by the demonstrable advantages of communistic management, by the growing spirit of brotherhood. But what has to be destroyed at once, even with violence if necessary, is *capitalistic property*—that is, the fact that a few control the natural wealth and the instruments of production and can thus oblige others to work for them.

ERRICO MALATESTA, *Umanità Nova,* April 18, 1922

We cry shame on the feudal baron who forbade the peasant to turn a clod of earth unless he surrendered to his lord a quarter of his crop. We called these the barbarous times. But if the forms have changed, the relations have remained the same, and the worker is forced, under the name of free contract, to accept feudal obligations. For, turn where he will, he can find no better conditions. Everything has become private property, and he must accept or die of hunger.

PETER KROPOTKIN, *The Conquest of Bread,* 1892

The misery of the workers arises from their being forced to produce for a crowd of parasites who turn the greater part of the products to their profit. If you are sincere, don't waste your time trying to conciliate antagonistic interests, don't look to ameliorate a situation that can produce nothing good: destroy parasitism. But one cannot wait for that to be done by individuals who are themselves only parasites, and it cannot be the work of a law; that is why it is necessary to destroy the system of exploitation and not ameliorate it.

JEAN GRAVE, *Dying Society and Anarchy,* 1893

In modern capitalism, exploitation rather than oppression is the real enemy of the people. Oppression is but its handmaid. Hence the battle is to be waged on the economic rather than the political field.

ALEXANDER BERKMAN, letter from prison, 1901

The principal reason for the bad exploitation of nature, the miseries of the workers, the antagonisms of the social struggles is the *right to property,* which confers on the owners of the land, the raw materials, and all the means of production the possibility of exploiting the labor of others and organizing production, not for the well-being of all, but to guarantee maximum profit for the owners. It is necessary, therefore, to abolish property.

ERRICO MALATESTA, *Umanità Nova,* May 10, 1922

If the present order cannot be defended on purely economic grounds, what possible justification can be made for it on the basis of human and social principles?

D. A. DE SANTILLAN, *After the Revolution,* 1936

The worker in England, France, Holland, and so on participates to some extent in the profits which, without effort on their part, fall into the laps of the bourgeoisie of his country from the unrestrained exploitation of colonial peoples; but sooner or later there comes a time when those people, too, wake up, and he has to pay all the more dearly for the small advantages he has enjoyed. Events in Asia will show this still more clearly in the near future.

RUDOLF ROCKER, *Anarcho-Syndicalism,* 1938

Real wealth consists in things of utility and beauty, in things that help to create strong, beautiful bodies and surroundings inspiring to live in. But if man is doomed to wind cotton around a spool, or dig coal, or build roads for thirty years of his life, there can be no talk of wealth. What he gives to the world is only gray and hideous things, reflecting a dull and hideous existence, too weak to live, too cowardly to die. Strange to say, there are people who extol this deadening method of centralized production as the proudest achievement of our age. They fail utterly to realize that if we are to continue in machine subserviency, our slavery is more complete than was our bondage to the King.

EMMA GOLDMAN, *Anarchism,* 1910

Man is being robbed not merely of the products of his labor, but of the power of free initiative or originality, and the interest in, or desire for, the things he is making.

EMMA GOLDMAN, *Anarchism,* 1910

Poverty will always exist! Yes, so long as property does.

P.-J. PROUDHON, *What Is Property?* 1840

The evil of the present system is . . . not that the "surplus-value" of production goes to the capitalist, as . . . Marx said . . . ; the surplus-value itself is but a consequence of deeper causes. The evil lies *in the possibility of a surplus-value existing,* instead of a simple surplus not consumed by each generation; for that a surplus-value should exist means that men, women, and children are compelled by hunger to sell their labor for a small part of what this labor produces.

PETER KROPOTKIN, *The Conquest of Bread,* 1892

It was poverty that created the first capitalist, because, before accumulating "surplus-value," of which we hear so much, men had to be sufficiently destitute to consent to sell their labor so as not to die of hunger. It was poverty that made capitalists.

PETER KROPOTKIN, *The Conquest of Bread,* 1892

Where industry is everything and man is nothing, there begins the domain of a ruthless economic despotism which is no less disastrous in its operation than any political despotism. The two despotisms strengthen each other and are fed from the same source.

RUDOLF ROCKER, preface to *Nationalism and Culture,* 1936

Capitalist monopoly is always and everywhere accompanied by the . . . extension of State centralization.

MICHAEL BAKUNIN, *Statism and Anarchy,* 1873

Private wealth was developed under the shadow of the ruling power, for its protection and—often unconsciously—as its accomplice. The class of proprietors arose and, concentrating little by little into their own hands all the means of production, the very fountains of life—agriculture, industry, and exchange—ended by becoming a power in themselves. This power, by the superiority of its means of action and the great mass of interests it embraces, always ends by subjugating more or less openly the political power—that is, the government—which it makes its policeman.

ERRICO MALATESTA, *Anarchy*, 1891

If you are a member of the propertied class, you can crawl out of anything you want to, for law is for sale; that is to say, whoever can purchase the lawyers, stock the jury, and bribe the court can win. There is only one law for the poor, to wit: Obey the rich.

ALBERT PARSONS, on being sentenced to hang, 1886

The legal right of the capitalist is virtually the assertion that one man has a greater right to life than another man, since it denies the equality of natural constitutions. Our present social system, therefore, is based upon the legalization of robbery, slavery and murder.

ALBERT PARSONS, on being sentenced to hang, 1886

Exploitation is the visible body, and government the soul, of the bourgeois regime.

MICHAEL BAKUNIN, *The Knouto-Germanic Empire,* 1871

Free! You are free—however, since you can live only by hiring out your productive force, and since those who employ it want nothing to be upset in the magnificent state of affairs that puts them in a position to exploit you—you who have dreamed of troubling such a beautiful social state, be free to drop dead of hunger, there will be no more work for you.

JEAN GRAVE, *Anarchy, Its Goal, Its Means,* 1899

Property—the god—also has its metaphysics. It is the science of the bourgeois economists. Like any metaphysics, it is a sort of twilight, a compromise between truth and falsehood, with the latter benefiting by it.

MICHAEL BAKUNIN, *The Knouto-Germanic Empire,* 1871

Much more seriously than they themselves realize, *property is [the bourgeoisie's] God,* their only God, which long ago replaced in their hearts the heavenly God of the Christians. And, like the latter in days of yore, the bourgeois are capable of suffering martyrdom and death for the sake of this God. The ruthless and desperate war they wage for the defense of property is not only a war of interests: it is a religious war in the full meaning of the word.

MICHAEL BAKUNIN, *The Knouto-Germanic Empire,* 1871

It is evident to anyone who wishes to see that productive work creates wealth and yields to the producer only poverty, and that it is only non-productive, exploiting labor that yields property. But since property is morality, it follows that *morality, as the bourgeois understand it, consists in exploiting someone else's labor.*

MICHAEL BAKUNIN, *The Knouto-Germanic Empire,* 1871

The teacher, the priest, and the preacher all imposed [the idea] upon you that your life is ordained by God and "His will be done." And when you saw a poor man dragged off to prison, they told you that he was bad because he had stolen something, and that it was a great crime.

But neither at home, nor in school, nor anywhere else were you ever told that it is a crime for the rich man to steal the product of the worker's labor, or that the capitalists are rich because they have possessed themselves of the wealth which labor created.

ALEXANDER BERKMAN, *What Is Communist Anarchism?* 1928

One must distinguish between the prejudices of the people and those of the privileged classes. The prejudices of the masses are based only on their ignorance and run counter to their own interests, where the prejudices of the bourgeoisie are based precisely on their interests. Which of the two is incurable? The bourgeoisie, without any doubt.

MICHAEL BAKUNIN, *The Politics of the International*, 1869

From Malthus on, conservatives of all schools have maintained that poverty does not result from unjust distribution of wealth, but from limited productivity or deficient human industry.

Socialism, in its historical origins and in its basic ethic, is the negation of this thesis; it is the clear statement that the social problem is above all a matter of social justice, a question of distribution.

ERRICO MALATESTA, *Il Pensiero*, May 16, 1905

Those who envision a society of well-stuffed pigs that waddle contentedly under the rod of a small number of swine-herds; who do not take into account the need for freedom and the sentiment of human dignity; who really believe in a god who orders, for his own abstruse ends, the poor to be submissive and the rich to be good and charitable—[those people] can also imagine and aspire to a technical age of production which assures abundance to all and is at the same time materially advantageous to both bosses and workers. But, in reality, "social peace" based on abundance for all will remain a dream as long as society is divided into antagonistic classes—that is, employers and employees. And there will be neither peace nor abundance.

ERRICO MALATESTA, *Umanità Nova*, May 10, 1922

In England, two prerequisites are attached to the right to be called a *gentleman:* he must go to church, but most of all he must own property. And the English language has a very forceful, picturesque, and naïve expression: *That man is worth so much*—that is to say, five, ten, or perhaps a hundred thousand pounds sterling. What the British (and the Americans) say in their grossly naïve manner, the bourgeoisie all over the world have in their thoughts. And the vast majority of the bourgeoisie—in Europe, America, Australia, in all the European colonies scattered throughout the world—is so convinced of this basic view that it never even suspects its deep immorality and inhumanity. The only thing that speaks in favor of the bourgeoisie is the very naïveté of this depravity.

MICHAEL BAKUNIN, *The Knouto-
Germanic Empire,* 1871

ABOLISH GOD

·

God is stupidity and cowardice; God is hypocrisy and false-hood; God is tyranny and poverty; God is evil. For as long as men bow before altars, mankind will remain damned, the slave of kings and priests. . . . Get thee hence, O God.

P.-J. PROUDHON, *System of Economic Contradictions*, 1846

We cannot, we ought not make the least concession to theology, because in that mystic and rigorously consistent alphabet, he who begins with A must fatally arrive at Z, and he who wants to adore God must renounce his liberty and his human dignity.

God exists; hence man is a slave.

Man is intelligent, just, free; hence God does not exist.

We defy anyone to avoid this circle; and now let all choose.

MICHAEL BAKUNIN, *Federalism, Socialism, and Anti-Theologism*, 1867

With all due deference to all the semi-philosophers and to all the so-called religious thinkers, we say: *The existence of*

God implies the abdication of human reason and justice; it is the negation of human liberty, and it necessarily ends in both theoretical and absolute slavery.

MICHAEL BAKUNIN, *Federalism, Socialism, and Anti-Theologism,* 1867

God being everything, the real world and man are nothing. God being truth, justice, and infinite life, man is falsehood, inequality, and death. God being master, man is the slave.

MICHAEL BAKUNIN, *God and the State,* 1871

For my part, I say that the first duty of the thinking, free man is ceaselessly to banish the idea of God from his mind and consciousness. For God, if he exists, is essentially hostile to our nature, and we in no way depend on his authority. . . . Each step in our progress represents one more victory in which we annihilate the Deity.

P.-J. PROUDHON, *System of Economic Contradictions,* 1846

I do not believe in God, because I believe in man. Whatever his mistakes, man has for thousands of years been working to undo the botched job your God has made.

EMMA GOLDMAN, speech to a church congregation, Detroit, 1897

Christianity is precisely the religion par excellence, because it exhibits and manifests to the fullest extent the very nature and essence of every religious system, which is *the impoverishment, enslavement, and annihilation of humanity for the benefit of divinity.*

MICHAEL BAKUNIN, *God and the State,* 1871

Whoever says revelation says revealers, messiahs, prophets, priests, and legislators inspired by God himself; and these,

once recognized as the representatives of divinity or truth,
. . . necessarily exercise absolute power.

MICHAEL BAKUNIN, *God and the State,* 1871

Divine morality is the absolute negation of human
morality.

MICHAEL BAKUNIN, *The Knouto-Germanic
Empire,* 1871

By what right could God still say to me: "Be holy even as I
am holy"? "Lying spirit" I would reply, "thou foolish God,
thy reign is past. Seek new victims among the beasts . . . .
Eternal father, Jupiter, Jehovah, we have learned to know
thy ways. Thou art, thou wast, and ever will be, the envier
of Adam and the tormentor of Prometheus.

P.-J. PROUDHON, *System of Economic
Contradictions,* 1846

We will not, therefore, lose our time praying to our imag-
inary God for things which our own exertions alone can
procure.

FRANCISCO FERRER, *The Origins and Ideals
of the Modern School,* 1913

Divine morality found its perfect expression in the Christian maxim: "Thou shalt love God more than thyself and
thou shalt love thy neighbor as much as thyself," which implies the sacrifice of both oneself, and one's neighbor to God.
One can admit the sacrifice of oneself, this being an obvious
act of sheer folly, but the sacrifice of one's fellow-man is from
the human point of view absolutely immoral. And why am I
forced toward this inhuman sacrifice? For the salvation of my
own soul; that is the last word of Christianity.

MICHAEL BAKUNIN, *The Knouto-Germanic
Empire,* 1871

If lies, ignorance, wickedness, and crime arise from that liberty that God bestows upon us, then God himself is a liar, ignorant, wicked, a criminal.

But to reconcile these two things—the existence of God and human liberty—is impossible. If God exists, he alone is free.

SEBASTIEN FAURE, *The Crimes of God,* 1906(?)

The individual in possession of his immortal soul and his inner liberty independent of society—the modern saint—has *material* need of society, without feeling the slightest need of society from a moral point of view.

But what should we call a relationship which, being motivated only by material needs, is not sanctioned or backed up by some moral need? Evidently there is only one name for it: *exploitation.*

MICHAEL BAKUNIN, *The Knouto-Germanic Empire,* 1871

Religion is a collective insanity, the more powerful because it is traditional folly, and because its origin is lost in the most remote antiquity.

MICHAEL BAKUNIN, *God and the State,* 1871

Whenever a chief of state speaks of God, be he William I, the Knouto-Germanic emperor, or [Ulysses S.] Grant, the President of the great republic, be sure that he is getting ready to shear once more his people-flock.

MICHAEL BAKUNIN, *God and the State,* 1871

With all due respects, then, to the metaphysicians and religious idealists, philosophers, politicians, and poets: *The idea of God implies the abdication of human reason and justice; it is the most decisive negation of human liberty, and necessarily ends in the enslavement of mankind, both in theory and in practice.*

MICHAEL BAKUNIN, *God and the State,* 1871

A jealous lover of human liberty, deeming it the absolute condition of all that we admire and respect in humanity, I reverse the phrase of Voltaire and say, *if God really existed, it would be necessary to abolish him.*

MICHAEL BAKUNIN, *God and the State,* 1871

People go to church as they go to a tavern, in order to stupefy themselves, to forget their misery, to see themselves in their imagination, for a few minutes at least, free and happy, as happy as others, the well-to-do people. Give them a human existence, and they will never go into a tavern or a church. And it is only the Social Revolution that can and will give them such an existence.

MICHAEL BAKUNIN, *A Circular Letter to My Friends in Italy,* October, 1871

All the religions with their gods were never anything but the creation of the credulous fancy of men who had not yet reached the level of pure reflection and free thought based upon science. Consequently, the religious Heaven was nothing but a mirage in which man, exalted by faith, long ago encountered his own image enlarged and reversed—that is, *deified.*

MICHAEL BAKUNIN, *Federalism, Socialism, and Anti-Theologism,* 1867

All religions are founded on blood, for all, as is known, rest essentially on the idea of sacrifice—that is, on the perpetual immolation of humanity to the insatiable vengeance of divinity. In this blood mystery, man is always the victim, and the priest—a man also, but one privileged by grace—is the divine executioner.

MICHAEL BAKUNIN, *Federalism, Socialism, and Anti-Theologism,* 1867

Everywhere . . . religious or philosophical idealism (the one being simply the more or less free interpretation of the other) serves today as the banner of bloody and brutal material force, of shameless material exploitation.

MICHAEL BAKUNIN, *The Knouto-Germanic Empire,* 1871

Revolt and passionate negation, theologically personified in the great and noble figure of Satan—there is the true emancipator of the human race in practice.

MICHAEL BAKUNIN, *The Political Theology of Mazzini* (fragment), 1871

.

REVOLUTION

.

HISTORY AND THE REVOLUTION

There is no power outside of man which can free him, none which can charge him with any "mission." Neither heaven nor history can do it. . . . It is not the "mission" but the interest of the proletariat to emancipate itself from bondage. If labor does not consciously and actively strive for it, it will never "happen." It is necessary to free ourselves from the stupid and false notion of "historic missions."

ALEXANDER BERKMAN, *What Is Communist Anarchism?* 1928

The last phase and the supreme goal of all human development is *liberty*. Jean-Jacques Rousseau and his disciples were wrong in seeking this liberty in the beginnings of history.

MICHAEL BAKUNIN, *Federalism, Socialism, and Anti-Theologism,* 1867

According to the materialist system, which is the only natural and logical system, society, far from limiting and detracting from the freedom of individuals, on the contrary, creates this freedom. *Society is the root and the tree, and*

93

freedom is its fruit. Consequently, in every epoch man has to seek his liberty, not at the beginning, but at the end of history, and one may say that the real and complete emancipation of every individual is the true and great objective and the supreme end of history.

MICHAEL BAKUNIN, *The Knouto-Germanic Empire,* 1871

Yes, our first ancestors, our Adams and our Eves, were, if not gorillas, very near relatives of gorillas, omnivorous, intelligent, and ferocious beasts, endowed in a higher degree than the animals of any other species with two precious faculties—*the power to think and the desire to rebel.*

These faculties, combining their progressive action in history, represent the essential factor, the negative power in the positive development of human animality, and create consequently all that constitutes humanity in man.

MICHAEL BAKUNIN, *God and the State,* 1871

Men, who are predominantly carnivorous animals, began their history with cannibalism. Now they aspire toward universal association, toward collective production and collective consumption of wealth.

But between these two extreme points—what a horrible and bloody tragedy! And we are not yet through with this tragedy.

MICHAEL BAKUNIN, *Letters on Patriotism,* 1869

Until now all human history has been only a perpetual and bloody immolation of millions of poor human beings in honor of some pitiless abstraction—God, country, power of State, national honor, historical rights, judicial rights, political liberty, public welfare.

MICHAEL BAKUNIN, *God and the State,* 1871

Like Nemesis of old, whom neither entreaty nor threats could move, revolution advances with inevitable and menacing tread on the flowers strewn before it by its devotees, through the blood of its defenders, and over the corpses of its enemies.

P.-J. PROUDHON, *The General Idea of Revolution in the Nineteenth Century,* 1851

The great evolution now taking place will be succeeded by the long-expected, the great revolution.

ELISÉE RECLUS, *Evolution and Revolution,* n.d.

The social revolution . . . is not an accident, not a sudden happening. There is nothing sudden about it, for ideas don't change suddenly. They grow slowly, gradually, like a plant or flower. Hence the social revolution is a result, a development, which means that it is revolutionary. It develops to the point where considerable numbers of people have embraced the new ideas and are determined to put them into practice. When they attempt to do so and meet with opposition, then the slow, quiet, and peaceful social evolution becomes quick, militant, and violent. Evolution becomes revolution.

ALEXANDER BERKMAN, *What Is Communist Anarchism?* 1928

Revolution is only an essential part of evolution, . . . no evolution is accomplished in nature without revolution. Periods of very slow changes are succeeded by periods of violent changes. Revolutions are as necessary for evolution as the slow changes which prepare them and succeed them.

PETER KROPOTKIN, *Revolutionary Studies,* 1892

Two things militate against gradual revolution: vested interests and the pride of the government.

P.-J. PROUDHON, *The General Idea of Revolution in the Nineteenth Century,* 1851

History does not wait for the idlers.

PETER KROPOTKIN, *Expropriation,* 1895 ed.

Those who would like to see society transformed without a jolt should abandon this notion; it is impossible . . . . Evolving ideas drive us to the revolution: one can regret it, deplore it, but the fact is there. . . . Since the revolution is inevitable, there is but one means of preventing it from turning against progress, and that is to take part in it and attempt to utilize it to achieve the ideal we have glimpsed.

JEAN GRAVE, *Dying Society and Anarchy,* 1893

To quarrel with socialism is silly and vain. To do so is to quarrel with history, to denounce the logic of events, to smother the aspirations of liberty.

ALBERT PARSONS, New York *Herald,* August 30, 1886

THE REVOLUTION

Ay, all of us together, we who suffer and are insulted daily, we are a multitude whom no man can number, we are the ocean that can embrace and swallow up all else.

When we have but the will to do it, that very moment will justice be done: that very instant the tyrants of the earth shall bite the dust.

PETER KROPOTKIN, *An Appeal to the Young,* 1880

We are revolutionaries because we believe that only the revolution, the violent revolution, can solve the social question. . . . We believe, furthermore, that the revolution is an act of will—the will of individuals and of the masses; that it needs for its success certain objective conditions, but that it does not happen of necessity, inevitably, through the single action of economic and political forces.

ERRICO MALATESTA, *Umanità Nova,* April 22, 1920

As long as there are rich and poor, governors and governed, there will be no peace, nor is it to be desired . . . ; for such a peace would be founded on the political, economic, and social inequality of millions of human beings who suffer hunger, outrages, prison, and death, while a small minority enjoys pleasures and liberties of all kinds for doing nothing. On with the struggle!

Manifesto of the Mexican Liberal Party
(Magonists), 1911

To those who think they can be really free only when their liberty ceases to trammel the liberty of the weakest of their fellows; to those who cannot be happy until they know that the pleasures in which they delight have not cost some disinherited one his tears, to them we say that there can be no holding back on the part of anyone who recognizes that one must struggle to be free.

JEAN GRAVE, *Anarchism and Its Practicality,* 1914

We believe that most of the ills that afflict mankind stem from a bad social organization; and that man could destroy them if he wished and knew how.

ERRICO MALATESTA, *Il Programma Anarchico,* 1920

Everything depends on what the people are capable of wanting.

ERRICO MALATESTA, *Il Programma Anarchico,* 1920

What brings people into the movement is not so much the material effects of modern economic life as a sense of outraged justice. The smallest wage struggle would be impossible without an ethical motive behind it. The stronger the sense of justice in the people, the more it influences their thoughts and actions.

RUDOLF ROCKER, *London Years,* 1956

Not all the misery we have in the world today comes from the lack of material welfare. Man can better stand starvation than the consciousness of injustice. The consciousness that you are treated unjustly will rouse you to protest and rebellion just as quickly as hunger, perhaps even quicker. Hunger may be the immediate cause of every rebellion or uprising, but beneath it is the slumbering antagonism and hatred of the masses against those at whose hands they are suffering injustice and wrong.

ALEXANDER BERKMAN, *What Is Communist Anarchism?* 1928

Reduced, intellectually and morally as well as materially, to the minimum of human existence, confined in their life like a prisoner in his prison, without horizon, without outlet, without even a future if we believe the economists, the people would have the singularly narrow souls and blunted instincts of the bourgeois if they did not feel a desire to escape; but of escape there are but three methods—two chimerical and a third real. The first two are the tavern and the church, debauchery of the body or debauchery of the mind; the third is social revolution.

MICHAEL BAKUNIN, *God and the State,* 1871

Misery, even joined to despair, is not sufficient to provoke the social revolution. . . . For that, an ideal is needed, which always arises historically from the depths of the instinct of the people, developed, broadened, and clarified by a series of marked events, difficult and bitter experiences. There must be, I say, a general idea of the people's rights and a profound, ardent, one might even say religious, faith in those rights. When that ideal and that faith are together in the people, side by side with the misery that pushes them to despair, then the social revolution is near, inevitable, and there is no force that can stop it.

MICHAEL BAKUNIN, *Statism and Anarchy,* 1873

In order to conquer, something more than guillotines is required. It is the revolutionary *idea,* the truly wide revolutionary conception, which reduces its enemies to impotence by paralyzing all the instruments by which they have governed hitherto.

PETER KROPOTKIN, *Revolutionary Studies,* 1892

Indispensable for the beginning of any revolution are, first of all, the realization of dissatisfaction with the present, the consciousness of the endlessness of this condition and of its irreparability by customary means, and finally, a readiness for risk in order to change this condition.

PETER KROPOTKIN, *Must We Occupy Ourselves . . . ?* 1873

The working class does not dream of adapting itself to the capitalist world, of fitting into the present system of production, in order to develop there in the best of its interests. It has higher aims—aims of social transformation—and it is these revolutionary aspirations which have led it to constitute itself as a class party, in opposition to all other parties and in opposition to all other classes.

EMILE POUGET, *The General Confederation of Labor,* 1908

Under the historical, juridical, religious, and social organization of most . . . countries, the economic emancipation of the workers is a sheer impossibility—and consequently, in order to attain and fully carry out that emancipation, it is necessary to destroy all modern institutions: the State, Church, Courts, University, Army and Police, all of which are ramparts erected by the privileged classes against the proletariat. And it is not enough to have them overthrown in one country only: it is essential to have them destroyed in all countries.

MICHAEL BAKUNIN, *Organization of the International,* 1871(?)

A revolution is, in the moral sphere, an act of sovereign justice that results from the force of circumstances. Consequently, it is its own justification, and it is a crime for a statesman to resist it.

P.-J. PROUDHON, *The General Idea of Revolution in the Nineteenth Century*, 1851

What do we understand by revolution? It is not a simple change of governors. It is the taking possession by the people of all social wealth. It is the abolition of all the forces which have so long hampered the development of humanity.

PETER KROPOTKIN, *Revolutionary Government*, 1892

Death to bourgeois society! Long live anarchy!

AUGUST VAILLANT, at his execution for throwing a bomb at the French Chamber of Deputies, 1894

Revolution breaks social forms grown too narrow for man. It bursts the molds which constrict him the more solidified they become, and the more Life, ever striving forward, leaves them. . . .

The abolition of the established—politically and economically, socially and ethically—the attempt to replace it with something different, is the reflex of man's changed needs, of the awakened consciousness of the people. Back of revolution are the millions of living humans who embody its inner spirit, who feel, think, and have their being in it.

ALEXANDER BERKMAN, *The Bolshevik Myth*, 1925

A revolution is a swift overthrow, in a few years, of institutions which have taken centuries to root in the soil, and seem so fixed and immovable that even the most ardent reformers hardly dare to attack them in their writings. It is the fall, the crumbling away in a brief period, of all that up to that time composed the essence of social, religious, political, and economic life in a nation. It means the subversion of acquired ideas and of accepted notions concerning each of the complex institutions and relations of the human herd.

In short, it is the birth of completely new ideas concerning the manifold links in citizenship—conceptions which soon become realities, and then begin to spread among the neighboring nations, convulsing the world. . . .

PETER KROPOTKIN, *The Great French Revolution*, 1909

A reform is always a compromise with the past, but the progress accomplished by revolution is always a promise of future progress.

PETER KROPOTKIN, *The Great French Revolution*, 1909

THE REVOLUTION CALLS FOR A NEW CIVILIZATION

We must overthrow the material and moral conditions of our present-day life. We must overthrow from top to bottom this effete social world, which has become impotent and sterile, and could not support or sustain so great a mass of freedom. . . . The social question takes the form primarily of the overthrow of society.

MICHAEL BAKUNIN, *Appeal to the Slavs*, first draft, 1848

While all Anarchists agree that the main evil today is an economic one, they maintain that the solution to that evil can be brought about only through the consideration of *every phase* of life, individual, as well as collective; the internal as well as the external phases.

EMMA GOLDMAN, *Anarchism*, 1910

Between man and the social environment there is a reciprocal action. Men make society what it is, and society makes men what they are, and the result is therefore a kind of vicious circle. To transform society, men must be changed, and to transform men, society must be changed.

Errico Malatesta, Il Programma Anarchico, 1920

The revolution is the creation of new living institutions, new groupings, new social relationships; it is the destruction of privileges and monopolies; it is the new spirit of justice, of brotherhood, of freedom which must renew the whole of social life and raise the moral level and material conditions of the masses by calling on them to provide, through direct and conscious action, for their own futures. Revolution is the organization of all public services by those who work in them in their own interest as well as the public's; revolution is the destruction of all coercive ties; it is the autonomy of groups, of communes, of regions; revolution is the free federation brought about by a desire for brotherhood, by individual and collective interests, by the needs of production and defense; revolution is the constitution of innumerable free groupings based on ideas, wishes, and tastes of all kinds that exist among the people; revolution is the forming and disbanding of thousands of representative, district, communal, regional, national bodies which, without having any legislative power, serve to make known and coordinate the desires and interests of people near and far and which act through information, advice, and example. Revolution is freedom proved through the crucible of facts.

Errico Malatesta, Pensiero e Volontà, June 15, 1924

We want to reconstruct Spain materially and morally. Our revolution will be both economic and ethical.

Tierra y Libertad, newspaper of the Anarchist
Federation of Iberia (FAI), 1936

The basic objective of our revolution is to restore to the people their rich wealth and culture. How? Materially, by expropriating capitalism. Morally, by distributing culture to those who have been deprived of it.

Program of the CNT, adopted at
Saragossa, May, 1936

To give full scope to socialism entails rebuilding from top to bottom a society dominated by the narrow individualism of the shopkeeper. It is not, as has sometimes been said by those indulging in metaphysical wooliness, just a question of giving the worker "the total product of his labor"; it is a question of completely reshaping all relationships, from those which exist today between every individual and his church-warden or his stationmaster to those which exist between neighborhoods, hamlets, cities, and regions.

PETER KROPOTKIN, *The State: Its Historic Role,* 1896

The social revolution, as the Latin and Slav toilers picture it to themselves, desire it, and hope for it, is infinitely broader than the revolution promised them by the German or Marxian program. For them it is not a question of the emancipation of the working class, parsimoniously measured out and realizable only at a very distant date, but of the complete and real emancipation of all the proletariat, not only of some countries but of all nations . . . a new civilization, genuinely of the people, destined to commence with this act of universal emancipation.

MICHAEL BAKUNIN, letter to *La Liberté,* October, 1872

To overturn a government, that is everything for a bourgeois revolutionary. For us, it is only the beginning of the social revolution. The State machine, once broken down, the hierarchy of functionaries fallen into disorganization and not knowing where to go, the soldiers having lost confidence in their leaders—in short, the army of the defenders of capital once thrown into rout—then we will address ourselves to the great work of demolishing the institutions that serve to perpetuate economic and political slavery.

PETER KROPOTKIN, *Words of a Rebel,* 1885

All political tenets and parties notwithstanding, no revolution can be truly and permanently successful unless it puts its emphatic veto upon all tyranny and centralization, and determinedly strives to make the revolution a real revaluation of all economic, social, and cultural values. Not mere substitution of one political party for another in the control of the Government, not the masking of autocracy by proletarian slogans, not the dictatorship of a new class over an old one, not political scene-shifting of any kind, but the complete reversal of these authoritarian principles will alone serve the revolution.

EMMA GOLDMAN, *My Disillusionment in Russia,* 1922

The social revolution means much more than the reorganization of conditions alone: it means the establishment of new human values and social relationships, a changed attitude of man to man, as of one free and independent to his equal; it means a different spirit in individual and collective life, and that spirit cannot be born overnight. It is a spirit to be cultivated and reared, as the most delicate flower is, for indeed it is the flower of a new and beautiful existence.

ALEXANDER BERKMAN, *What Is Communist Anarchism?* 1928

[Revolution] is the herald of NEW VALUES, ushering in a transformation of the basic relations of man to man, and of man to society. It is not a mere reformer, patching up some social evils; not a mere changer of forms and institutions; not only a redistributor of social well-being, It is all that, yet more, much more. It is, first and foremost, the TRANS-VALUATOR, the bearer of *new* values. It is the great TEACHER of the NEW ETHICS, inspiring man with a new concept of life and its manifestations in social relationships. It is the mental and spiritual regenerator. . . .

Applied in practice, it means that the period of the actual revolution, the so-called transitory stage, must be the introduction, the prelude to the new social conditions. It is the threshold to the NEW LIFE, the new HOUSE OF MAN AND HUMANITY. As such it must be of the spirit of the new life, harmonious with the construction of the new edifice.

EMMA GOLDMAN, *My Further Disillusionment in Russia,* 1922

To forget ethical values, to introduce practices and methods inconsistent with or opposed to the high moral purposes of the revolution, means to invite counterrevolution and disaster.

ALEXANDER BERKMAN, *What Is Communist Anarchism?* 1928

In my opinion—a thousandfold strengthened by the Russian experience—the great mission of revolution, of the SOCIAL REVOLUTION, is the *fundamental transvaluation of values.* A transvaluation not only of social, but also of human values. The latter are even preeminent, for they are the basis of all social values.

EMMA GOLDMAN, *My Further Disillusionment in Russia,* 1922

The anarchist revolution that we want goes well beyond the interests of a class: it proposes the complete liberation of humanity now enslaved from the triple point of view—economic, political, and moral.

ERRICO MALATESTA, speech before the Congress of the Anarchist International, Amsterdam, 1907

The day on which old institutions will fall under the proletarian ax, voices will cry out: "Bread, shelter, ease for all!" And those voices will be listened to; the people will say; "Let us begin by allaying our thirst for life, for happiness, for liberty, that we have never quenched. And when we shall have tasted of this joy, we will set to work to demolish the last vestiges of middle-class rule: its morality drawn from account books, its 'debit and credit' philosophy, its 'mine and yours' institutions. 'In demolishing we shall build,' as Proudhon said, and we shall build in the name of Communism and Anarchy."

PETER KROPOTKIN, *The Conquest of Bread*, 1892

It cannot be sufficiently emphasized that revolution is in vain unless inspired by its ultimate ideal. . . .

The ethical values which the revolution is to establish in the new society must be *initiated* with the revolutionary activities of the so-called transitional period. The latter can serve as a real and dependable bridge to the better life only if built of the same material as the life to be achieved. Revolution is the mirror of the coming day; it is the child that is to be the Man of Tomorrow.

EMMA GOLDMAN, *My Further Disillusionment
in Russia,* 1922

Liberated from the degrading and brutalizing struggle for our daily bread, all sharing in labor and well-being, the best qualities of man's heart and mind would have opportunity for growth and beneficial application. Man would indeed become the noble work of nature that he has till now envisioned himself only in his dreams.

ALEXANDER BERKMAN, *What Is Communist
Anarchism?* 1928

Life in freedom, in anarchy, will do more than liberate man from his present political and economic bondage. That will be only the first step, the preliminary to a truly human existence. Far greater and more significant will be the *results* of such liberty, its effects upon man's mind, upon his personality. The abolition of the coercive external will, and with it the fear of authority, will loosen the bonds of moral compulsion no less than of economic and physical. Man's spirit will breathe freely, and that mental emancipation will be the birth of a new culture, a new humanity.

ALEXANDER BERKMAN, *What Is Communist Anarchism?* 1928

By flinging overboard law, religion, and authority, mankind can regain possession of the moral principle which has been taken from them. Regain that they may criticize it, and purge it from the adulteration wherewith priest, judge, and ruler have poisoned it and are poisoning it yet.

PETER KROPOTKIN, *Anarchist Morality,* 1909

We are not in the least afraid of ruins. We are going to inherit the earth; there is not the slightest doubt about that. The bourgeoisie might blast and ruin its own world before it leaves the stage of history. We carry a new world here in our hearts. That world is growing this minute.

BUENAVENTURA DURRUTI, interview with the Toronto *Star* during the Spanish Civil War, September, 1936

We will conquer, not so that we may follow the example of past years and hand over our fate to some new master, but to take it in our hands and conduct our lives according to our own will and our own conceptions of truth.

NESTOR MAKHNO, proclamation to the Ukrainian Peasants, 1918

Once the violent aspect of the revolution has ended, we will abolish: private property, the State, the principle of authority, and consequently, the classes that divide men into exploiters and exploited, oppressors and oppressed.

Program of the CNT, adopted at Saragossa, May, 1936

"DESTRUCTION IS THE BEGINNING
OF CONSTRUCTION"

There can be no revolution without a sweeping and passionate destruction, since by means of such destruction new worlds are born and come into existence.

MICHAEL BAKUNIN, *Statism and Anarchy,* 1873

Destructive action is ever determined—not only its essence and the degree of its intensity, but likewise the means it uses—by the positive ideal which constitutes its initial inspiration, its soul.

MICHAEL BAKUNIN, *Protestation of the Alliance,* 1871

Violence is justifiable only when it is necessary to defend oneself and others from violence. It is where necessity ceases that crime begins. . . .

The slave is always in a state of legitimate defense, and consequently his violence against the boss, against the oppressor, is always morally justifiable and must be controlled only by such considerations as that the best and most economical use is being made of human effort and human sufferings.

ERRICO MALATESTA, *Umanità Nova,* August 25, 1921

Our high ideal is not violence but peace, a society of people who are free and equal, in which conflicts and massacres will be impossible. Violence is not ours but theirs, of the governing class, which oppresses, tramples, and murders the weaker. There is nothing left to the proletariat but to react violently against their violence and to put lead against lead to crush violence.

ERRICO MALATESTA, funeral oration for five Italian workers slain by gendarmes and nationalists, 1920

Do you mean to destroy?

Do you mean to build?

These are the questions we have been asked from many quarters, by inquirers sympathetic and otherwise.

Our reply is frank and bold: to destroy *and* to build.

For, socially speaking, Destruction is the beginning of Construction.

Superficial minds speak sneeringly of destruction. Oh, it is easy to destroy, they say, but to build, to build, that's the important work!

It's nonsense. No structure, social or otherwise, can endure if built on a foundation of lies.

Before the garden can bloom, the weeds must be uprooted. Nothing is more important than to destroy. Nothing more necessary and more difficult.

ALEXANDER BERKMAN, *The Blast*, January 15, 1916

There is only one way to make a political force harmless, to pacify and subdue it, and that is to proceed with its destruction.

MICHAEL BAKUNIN, *Statism and Anarchy*, 1873

The revolution must of necessity be violent, even though violence is itself an evil. It must be violent because it would be folly to hope that the privileged classes will recognize the injustice of, the harm caused by, their privileged status, and will voluntarily renounce it. It must be violent because a transitional, revolutionary violence is the only way to put an end to the far greater, the permanent, violence that keeps the majority of mankind in servitude.

ERRICO MALATESTA, *Umanità Nova*, August 12, 1920

The Revolution is often associated with a sense of catastrophe as a natural result of the fear of the privileged few—the minority that expropriates the toil of others. But—serious as the damage of civil war would be—the harm could never be so great as the misery wrought in a normal, perfectly peaceful year under capitalism.

D. A. DE SANTILLAN, *After the Revolution,* 1936

We want to expropriate the property-owning class, and with violence, since it is with violence that they hold onto social wealth and use it to exploit the working class. Not because freedom is a good thing for the future, but because it is a good thing at all times, today as well as tomorrow. The property owners, by denying us the means of exercising our freedom, in effect take it away from us.

We want to overthrow the government, all governments— and overthrow them with violence since it is by the use of violence that they force us to obey—and, once again . . . because governments are the negation of freedom and it is not possible to be free without being rid of them.

By force we want to deprive the priests of their privileges, because with these privileges, secured by the power of the State, they deny others the right, that is, the means, of equal freedom to propagate their ideas and beliefs.

ERRICO MALATESTA, *La Questione Sociale,*
November 25, 1899

I think that the oppressed are always in a state of legitimate self-defense and have always the right to attack the oppressors. I admit, therefore, that there are wars that are necessary, holy wars: and there are wars of liberation, such as are generally called "civil wars"—that is, revolutions.

ERRICO MALATESTA, *Anarchists Have
Forgotten Their Principles,* 1914

Revolutions are not child's play, nor are they academic debates in which only vanities are hurt in furious clashes, nor literary jousts wherein only ink is spilled profusely. Revolution means war, and that implies the destruction of men and things. Of course, it is a pity that humanity has not yet invented a more peaceful means of progress, but until now every forward step in history has been achieved only after it has been baptized in blood. For that matter, reaction can hardly reproach revolution on this point; it has always shed more blood than the latter.

MICHAEL BAKUNIN, *The Bear of Berne and the Bear of St. Petersburg,* 1870

Most people have very confused notions about revolution. To them it means just fighting, smashing things, destroying. It is the same as if rolling up your sleeves for work should be considered as the work itself that you have to do. The fighting part of revolution is merely the rolling up of your sleeves. The real, actual tasks are ahead.

ALEXANDER BERKMAN, *What Is Communist Anarchism?* 1928

Anarchists are opposed to violence. . . . The main plank of anarchism is the removal of violence from human relations. It is life based on the freedom of the individual, without the intervention of the police. For this reason we are enemies of capitalism, which depends on the protection of the police to force workers to allow themselves to be exploited. . . . We are therefore enemies of the State, which is the coercive, violent organization of society.

ERRICO MALATESTA, *Umanità Nova,* August 25, 1921

It was in the name of equality that the bourgeoisie overthrew and massacred the nobility. And it is in the name of equality that we now demand either the violent death or the voluntary suicide of the bourgeoisie, only with this difference—that being less bloodthirsty than the bourgeoisie of the revolutionary period, we do not want the death of men but the abolition of positions and things.

MICHAEL BAKUNIN, *The Lullers,* 1868–69

Anarchists propose to "crop off the head" of the private-property beast. . . . It is more than probable, however, that in the effort to slay this "monster" it will be necessary to "crop off" the heads of a large number of its progeny (capitalists), who will stoutly defend the life of their parent.

ALBERT PARSONS, The Kansas *Lucifer,* 1885

The struggle against government is, in the last analysis, physical, material. . . .
The only limit to the oppression of government is the power with which the people show themselves capable of opposing it.

ERRICO MALATESTA, *Il Programma Anarchico,* 1920

Socialists will not be able to prevent the people in the early days of the Revolution from giving vent to their fury by doing away with a few hundred of the most odious, the most rabid and dangerous enemies. But once that hurricane passes, the Socialists will oppose with all their might hypocritical—in a political and juridical sense—butchery perpetrated in cold blood.

MICHAEL BAKUNIN, *A Circular Letter to My Friends in Italy,* October, 1871.

You can't destroy wage slavery by wrecking the machinery in the mills and factories, can you? You can't destroy government by setting fire to the White House.
To think of revolution in terms of violence and destruction is to misinterpret and falsify the whole idea of it. In practical application such a conception is bound to lead to disastrous results.
When a great thinker like the famous anarchist Bakunin speaks of revolution as destruction, he has in mind the idea of authority and obedience which are to be destroyed. It is for this reason that he said destruction means construction, for to destroy a false belief is indeed most constructive work.

ALEXANDER BERKMAN, *What Is Communist Anarchism?* 1928

To make a radical revolution, it is necessary to attack positions and things, to destroy property and the State, and then there will be no need to destroy men and to be condemned to the infallible and inevitable reaction that never has failed and never will fail to produce the massacre of men in each society.

But for men to have the right to be humane, without danger to the revolution, it will be necessary to be pitiless to positions and things; it will be necessary to destroy everything, above all and before all, property and its inevitable corollary: the State. That is the secret of the Revolution.

MICHAEL BAKUNIN, *Program and Object of the Secret Revolutionary Organization of International Brothers,* 1868

There may be cases where passive resistance is an effective weapon, and it would then obviously be the best of weapons, since it would be the most economical in human suffering. But more often than not, to profess passive resistance only serves to reassure the oppressors against their fear of rebellion, and thus it betrays the cause of the oppressed.

It is interesting to observe how both the *terrorists* and the *tolstoyans* [pacifists]—just because both are mystics—arrive at practical results that are more or less similar. The former would not hesitate to destroy half of mankind so long as the idea triumphed; the latter would be prepared to let all mankind remain under the yoke of great suffering rather than violate a principle.

ERRICO MALATESTA, *Anarchia,* August, 1896

Since the environment today, which obliges the masses to live in misery, is maintained by violence, we advocate and prepare for violence. That is why we are revolutionaries, and not because "we are desperate men, thirsting for revenge and filled with hate."

ERRICO MALATESTA, *Umanità Nova,*
September 30, 1920

Workingmen of America, learn the manufacture and use of dynamite. It will be your most powerful weapon; a weapon of the weak against the strong. . . . Then use it unstintingly, unsparingly. The battle for bread is the battle for life. . . . Death and destruction to the system and its upholders, which plunders and enslaves the men, women, and children of toil.

The Chicago *Alarm,* November 8, 1884

Dynamite! Of all the good stuff, this is the stuff. Stuff several pounds of this sublime stuff into an inch pipe (gas or water-pipe), plug up both ends, insert a cap with a fuse attached, place this in the immediate neighborhood of a lot of rich loafers who live by the sweat of other people's brows, and light the fuse. A most cheerful and gratifying result will follow. In giving dynamite to the downtrodden millions of the globe, science has done its best work. . . . It is a formidable weapon against any force of militia, police, or detectives that may want to stifle the cry for justice that goes forth from the plundered slaves. It is something not very ornamental but exceedingly useful. . . . It is a genuine boon for the disinherited, while it brings terror and fear to the robbers. . . . A pound of this good stuff beats a bushel of ballots all hollow, and don't you forget it. Our lawmakers might as well try to sit down on a crater of a volcano.

Letter from an Indianapolis member of the *International* to the Chicago *Alarm,* February 21, 1885

Dynamite is the diffusion of power. It is democratic; it makes everybody equal. . . . Nothing can meet it. The Pinkertons, the police, the militia are absolutely worthless in the presence of dynamite. . . . It is the equilibrium. It is the annihilator. It is the disseminator of power. It is the downfall of oppression. It is the abolition of authority; it is the dawn of peace; it is the end of war, because war cannot exist unless there is somebody to make war upon, and dynamite makes that unsafe.

ALBERT PARSONS, on being sentenced to hang, 1886

One must not think of destroying everything in the belief that, later, things will look after themselves.

ERRICO MALATESTA, *Pensiero e Volontà,* October 1, 1925

Terror has always been the instrument of tyranny. . . . Those who believe in the liberating and revolutionary efficacy of repression and savagery have the same kind of backward mentality as the jurists who believe that crimes can be prevented and the world morally improved by the imposition of stiff punishments.

ERRICO MALATESTA, *Pensiero e Volontà,* October 1, 1924

It cannot and it shall not be denied that most anarchists feel convinced that the development of the present social order cannot be brought upon its right track by peaceable proceedings only. But that is a question of tactics which has nothing to do with principles.

JOHANN MOST, *The Social Monster,* 1890

The anarchists . . . have no lust for murder and incendiarism. But they carry on a revolutionary agitation because they know that the power of a privileged class has never yet been broken by peaceable means.

JOHANN MOST, *The Social Monster,* 1890

We have preached dynamite. Yes, we have predicted from the lessons history teaches that the ruling classes of today would no more listen to the voice of reason than their predecessors; that they would attempt by brute force to stay the wheel of progress. Is it a lie, or was it the truth we told?

AUGUST SPIES, on being sentenced to hang, 1886

If they use cannons against us, we shall use dynamite against them.

LOUIS LINGG, courtroom speech, Chicago, 1886

The anarchists think that the destruction of capitalist and authoritarian society can be realized only by armed insurrection and violent expropriation and that the use of the general strike and the trade union movement should not make us forget the most direct means of struggle against the military force of the governments.

The International Anarchist Congress,
Amsterdam, 1907

During revolutionary periods, as in Russia, the act of revolt serves a double goal without considering its psychological character: it undermines the base of tyranny and raises the enthusiasm of the timid. This is the case, above all, when terrorist activity is directed against the most brutal and hated agents of despotism.

The International Anarchist Congress,
Amsterdam, 1907

Anarchists have no monopoly on violence. On the contrary, the teachings of anarchism are those of peace and harmony, of noninvasion, of the sacredness of life and liberty. But anarchists are human, like the rest of mankind, and perhaps more so. They are more sensitive to wrong and injustice, quicker to resent oppression, and therefore not exempt from occasionally voicing their protest by an act of violence. But such acts are an expression of individual temperament, not of any particular theory.

ALEXANDER BERKMAN, *What Is Communist Anarchism?* 1928

I am sick of this rottenness and sham. I know that all life under capitalism is violence; that every instant of its existence spells murder and bloodshed. Every one of you who defends the present system knows it. Every one of you is guilty, openly and secretly, of violence and outrage in the protection of *his* interests. Well, since you have driven labor to this necessity, it defends *its* interests with the weapons *you* use against it, the weapons you force upon it. . . .

ALEXANDER BERKMAN, *Mother Earth,* November, 1911

Has a single step been made on the road of progress without violence and bloodshed? Has capital ever granted concessions without being forced to it? Has labor won aught but defeat and humiliation in the arena of legality? Away with deceit and cant! As long as you uphold the capitalist system of murder and robbery, just so long will labor resort to violence to wrest better terms. And the sooner we gain the courage to face the situation honestly, the speedier will come the day when the arch-crime of the centuries—Capitalism— the source and breeder of all other crime and violence, will be abolished and the way cleared for a society based on the solidarity of interests, where brotherhood and humanity will become a reality and violence disappear, because unnecessary.

ALEXANDER BERKMAN, *Mother Earth,* November, 1911

Long live the revolution! Long live anarchy!

SANTO CASERIO, as he stabbed the President of France, 1894

The workers in arms are the sole guarantee of the Revolution. To attempt to disarm the workers is to put oneself on the other side of the barricade. However much of a Councillor and Commissar one may be, one cannot dictate orders to the workers who are struggling against fascism with more sacrifice and heroism than all the politicians of the rearguard, whose capriciousness and impotence no one can ignore. Workers: let no one allow himself to be disarmed.

CNT, *Solidaridad Obrera,* Barcelona, May 2, 1937

Of course we do not wish to lay a finger on anyone; we would wish to dry all the tears of humanity and not be responsible for more tears. But we must either struggle in the world as it is or remain helpless dreamers.

ERRICO MALATESTA, *l'En Dehors,* August 17, 1892

ANARCHISM STANDS FOR DIRECT ACTION

We anarchists do not want to *emancipate* the people: we want the people to *emancipate themselves.*

ERRICO MALATESTA, *l'Agitazione,* June 18, 1897

How is it that men who only yesterday [in France in 1789] were complaining quietly of their lot as they smoked their pipes, and the next moment were humbly saluting the local guard and gendarme whom they had just been abusing—how is it that these same men a few days later were capable of seizing their scythes and their iron-shod pikes and attacking in his castle the lord who only yesterday was so formidable? By what miracle were these men . . . transformed in a day into heroes, marching through bullets and cannonballs to the conquest of their rights? . . .

The answer is easy.

Action, the continuous action, ceaselessly renewed, of minorities brings about this transformation. Courage, devotion, the spirit of sacrifice are as contagious as cowardice, submission, and panic.

PETER KROPOTKIN, *The Spirit of Revolt,* 1880

When a revolutionary situation arises in a country, before the spirit of revolt is sufficiently awakened in the masses to express itself in violent demonstrations in the streets or by rebellions and uprisings, it is through *action* that minorities succeed in awakening that feeling of independence and that spirit of audacity without which no revolution can come to a head.

PETER KROPOTKIN, *The Spirit of Revolt,* 1880

The Italian Federation believes that the insurrectionary deed, which attempts to affirm socialist principles by action, is the most efficient means of propaganda, the only one which, neither cheating nor depraving the masses, is able to direct the living forces of mankind toward support of the international struggle.

ERRICO MALATESTA, letter to Cafiero, December, 1876

Direct Action, that is the worker's Force in creative labor: that is the Forces giving birth to the new right—making the social right!

Force is the origin of all movement, of all action and, necessarily, it is the crowning of it. Life is the blossoming of Force and, outside of Force, there is nothing. Outside of it, nothing is manifested, nothing materializes.

EMILE POUGET, prison writing, 1909

There is no greater fallacy than the belief that aims and purposes are one thing, while methods and tactics are another.

EMMA GOLDMAN, *My Further Disillusionment in Russia,* 1922

By direct action the Anarcho-Syndicalists mean every method of immediate warfare by the workers against their economic and political oppressors. Among these, the outstanding are the strike, in all its gradations from the simple wage-struggle to the general strike; the boycott; sabotage in its countless forms; anti-militarist propaganda; and in particularly critical cases, . . . armed resistance of the people for the protection of life and liberty.

RUDOLF ROCKER, *Anarcho-Syndicalism,* 1938

Anarcho-Syndicalists . . . are not in any way opposed to the political struggle, but in their opinion this struggle, too, must take the form of direct action, in which the instruments of economic power that the working class has at its command are the most effective.

RUDOLF ROCKER, *Anarcho-Syndicalism,* 1938

Anarchism . . . stands for direct action, the open defiance of, and resistance to, all laws and restrictions, economic, social, and moral. But defiance and resistance are illegal. Therein lies the salvation of man.

EMMA GOLDMAN, *Anarchism,* 1910

Direct action, while proclaiming the inevitable use of force, prepares the ruin of the regimes of force and violence, so as to substitute for them a society of conscience and concord. . . .

Direct action, besides its value of social fruitfulness, carries in it a value of moral fruitfulness, because it refines and elevates those whom it impregnates, frees them from the weight of passivity, and incites them to spread in force and in beauty.

EMILE POUGET, *The Character of Direct Action,* 1908

A law is bad; the people consider it bad. Well, there is no necessity for petitions and speeches if people are really in earnest. Disobey it! Disobey it in force and that law will be heard of no more.

Direct action, after all, simply means that each of us individually must decide for himself the morality of any course of action.

J. BLAIR SMITH, *Direct Action Versus
Legislation,* 1899(?)

The communes of the next revolution will proclaim and establish their independence by direct socialist revolutionary action [and] abolish private property. When the revolutionary situation ripens, which may happen any day, and governments are swept aside by the people, when the middle-class camp, which only exists by State protection, is thus thrown into disorder, the insurgent people will not wait until some new government decrees, in its marvelous wisdom, a few economic reforms. The people themselves will abolish private property by a violent expropriation, taking possession in the name of the whole community of all the wealth accumulated by the labor of past generations.

PETER KROPOTKIN, *The Commune of Paris,* 1880

There are at this time, if I do not deceive myself, five principal currents in Anarchy which tend, each of them, to accomplish a number of things. . . .

1. First, and first in date, . . . refusal of military service.

2. Another style of activity . . . which has begun to haunt the mind of anarchists is the desire to create colonies, groupments, where the anarchist cells would try to live—as much as can be done, in the present social order—in a manner conforming as much as possible to their ways of thinking.

3. The question of workers, trade unionism, cooperatives, . . . several comrades are tending to return there, sensing that there are things to do.

4. On the side of education, the wish to rub out bourgeois education, which deforms the brains of our children.

and 5. Propaganda in the countryside, . . . where there is much to do.

JEAN GRAVE, *Anarchy, Its Goal, Its Means,* 1899

The anarchist idea, which already has increased the number of acts of insubordination [in the Army], is growing and will yet increase them even more. And then, when a considerable number of draftees take the path of exile to foreign countries instead of that to the barracks, what will the State do?

. . . So long as acts of insubordination remain isolated, those who do them, if they want to remain at liberty, are forced to flee or to hide, but when these acts are numerous, they will create an atmosphere favorable to them. Then, instead of fleeing or hiding, they will begin to struggle against the policeman.

JEAN GRAVE, *Anarchy, Its Goal, Its Means,* 1899

To act for oneself, counting only on oneself, that is what direct action is. It goes without saying, such action would take diverse forms.

PIERRE MONATTE, at the Congress of the
Anarchist International, 1907

Political action leads to capitalism reformed. Direct action leads to socialism. . . .

E. J. HIGGINS, *Mother Earth,* April, 1912

My conception of the strike of the future is not to strike and go out and starve, but to strike and remain in and take possession of the necessary property of production. If anyone is to starve . . . let it be the capitalist class.

LUCY PARSONS, speech at the first I.W.W.
convention, 1905

It is only those who do nothing who make no mistakes.

PETER KROPOTKIN, *Anarchism: Its Philosophy
and Ideal,* n.d.

EXPROPRIATION

From the first day of the revolution the worker shall know that a new era is opening before him; that henceforwards none need crouch under the bridges while palaces are hard by, none need fast in the midst of plenty, none need perish with cold near shops full of furs; that all is for all, in practice as well as in theory, and that at last, for the first time in history, a revolution has been accomplished which considers the NEEDS of the people before schooling them in their duties. This cannot be brought about by acts of parliament, but only by taking immediate and effective possession of all that is necessary to ensure the well-being of all; this is the only really scientific way of going to work, the only way which can be understood and desired by the mass of the people.

PETER KROPOTKIN, *The Conquest of Bread*, 1892

A general expropriation alone can satisfy the multitude of sufferers and oppressed . . . but, in order that expropriation may correspond with its principle, which is the suppression of private property and the restoration of all to all, it ought to be accomplished in vast proportions. On a small scale it would seem only vulgar pillage; on a large scale it would be the commencement of the Social Revolution.

PETER KROPOTKIN, *Expropriation*, 1887

If one really wants to change the system in fact and not just superficially, it will be necessary to destroy capitalism *de facto*, expropriating those who now control all social wealth, and immediately set about organizing a new social life on a local basis and without passing through legal channels. This means to say that in order to create a "social republic" one must first bring about . . . Anarchy!

ERRICO MALATESTA, *Umanità Nova*, April 1, 1920

A revolution, from its very outset, must be an act of justice toward "the downtrodden and the oppressed," not a promise of such reparation later on; otherwise, it is sure to fail. Unfortunately, it often happens that the leaders are so much absorbed with mere questions of military tactics that they forget the main thing. For revolutionists not to succeed in proving to the masses that a new era has really begun for them is to ensure the certain failure of their cause.

PETER KROPOTKIN, *Memoirs of a Revolutionist*, 1899

As a first step in the Revolution, we are concerned with the taking possession of the whole economic structure and its direct administration by the producers themselves, in order to assure the satisfaction of the fundamental necessities of the people.

D. A. DE SANTILLAN, *After the Revolution,* 1936

The matter of taking over the industries is not something that can be left to chance, nor can it be carried out in a haphazard manner. It can be accomplished only in a . . . systematic and organized way. You alone can't do it, nor I, nor any other man, be he worker, Ford, or the Pope of Rome. There is no man or any body of men that can manage it except the *workers themselves,* for it takes the workers to operate the industries.

ALEXANDER BERKMAN, *What Is Communist Anarchism?* 1928

The expropriation of dwellings contains in germ the whole social revolution. On the manner of its accomplishment depends the character of all that follows. Either we shall start on a good road leading straight to anarchist communism, or we shall remain sticking in the mud of despotic individualism.

PETER KROPOTKIN, *Conquest of Bread,* 1892

Once legal protection has been removed from property, the workers will have to take possession of all land that is not being directly cultivated by the existing owners with their own hands; they will have to form associations and organize production. . . . Agreements will promptly be reached with the associations of industrial workers for the exchange of goods, either on a communistic basis or in accordance with the criteria prevailing in different localities.

ERRICO MALATESTA, *Umanità Nova,* May 15, 1920

In order that the Revolution be something more than a name, and that a reaction may not bring us back on the morrow to the situation of the day before, it is necessary that the conquest of the day should be worth defending; it is necessary that he who was wretched yesterday should no longer be miserable today.

PETER KROPOTKIN, *Expropriation,* 1887

If the revolution immediately puts expropriation into effect, it will receive an interior thrust that will permit it to resist both the attempts to form a government which will seek to strangle it as well as attacks from the outside.

PETER KROPOTKIN, report to the Jura Workers' Federation, 1879

Grasp this part, my friend. The expropriation of the capitalist class during the social revolution—the taking over of the industries—requires tactics directly the reverse of those you now use in a strike. In the latter you quit work and leave the boss in full possession of the mill, factory, or mine. It is an idiotic proceeding, of course, for you give the master the entire advantage: he can put scabs in your place, and you remain out in the cold.

In expropriating, on the contrary, you *stay* on the job and put the boss out. He may remain only on equal terms with the rest: a worker among workers.

ALEXANDER BERKMAN, *What Is Communist Anarchism?* 1928

The social revolution, wherever it breaks out, must consider as its first duty the increase of production.

PETER KROPOTKIN, *Words of a Rebel,* 1919 edition

The slogan of the International was, you will remember, *the emancipation of the workers will be the task of the workers themselves*—and this is still our slogan, for we are the partisans of direct action and the adversaries of parliamentarism.

PIERRE MONATTE, speech at the Congress of the Anarchist International, Amsterdam, 1907

We have said, and we will never cease to repeat it: no go-betweens, no brokers and obliging servants who always end up as the true masters; we want all the existing wealth to be *seized directly* by the people themselves, to be guarded in their powerful hands, and we want the people themselves to decide on the best manner of enjoying it, be it for production or for consumption.

CARLO CAFIERO, *Anarchy and Communism,* 1880

THE ANARCHISTS

·

THE ROLE OF THE ANARCHISTS

We know that in politics there is no useful and honest practice possible without a theory and without a clearly determined goal. Otherwise, inspired as we are with the largest and most liberal feelings, we might end up with a reality diametrically opposite to those feelings: we might begin with convictions that are republican, democratic, and socialist—and finish as Bismarckians or as Bonapartists.

MICHAEL BAKUNIN, *Federalism, Socialism,*
and Anti-Theologism, 1867

This revolution is not only a theoretical conception; it is in the nature of things. It is the development of the current situation that will drive it. However, if the situation is the principal . . . lever of the revolution, the . . . intelligent and appropriate intervention of the party that possesses the theoretical conception of this revolution is not for that reason a less important factor. Hence, we must not wait for the revolution to fall from the sky but we must prepare it within the limits of the possible. Above all, we must ensure in this way that the revolution does not turn anew to the advantage of the governing classes.

Workers' Federation of the District of Courtelary, 1880

Our task is that of "pushing" the people to demand and to seize all the freedom they can and to make themselves responsible for providing for their own needs without waiting for orders from any kind of authority. Our task is that of demonstrating the uselessness and harmfulness of government, of provoking and encouraging by propaganda and action all kinds of individual and collective initiatives.

ERRICO MALATESTA, *l'Adunata dei Refrattari,*
December 26, 1931

All that individuals can do is elaborate, clarify, and propagate ideas corresponding to the popular instinct and contribute their incessant efforts to the revolutionary organization of the natural power of the masses; . . . the rest can and should be done by the masses themselves.

MICHAEL BAKUNIN, *The Paris Commune
and the Notion of the State,* 1871

For the triumph of the revolution against the reaction, it is necessary that, in the atmosphere of popular anarchy that will constitute the life and energy of the revolution, unity of thought and revolutionary action should find an organ. That organ must be the secret and universal association of the International Brothers.

The only thing that can make a well-organized society is to aid in the birth of a revolution by spreading among the masses ideas corresponding to their own instincts and by organizing, not the army of the revolution—the army must always be the people—but a sort of revolutionary staff, composed of devoted, energetic, intelligent, and above all sincere individuals of the people, not ambitious nor vain, capable of serving as intermediaries between the revolutionary idea and the instincts of the people.

MICHAEL BAKUNIN, *Program and Object of the Secret Revolutionary Organization of International Brothers*, 1868

The first condition of victory by the people is *agreement among the people* or *organization* of the people's forces.

MICHAEL BAKUNIN, *Science and the Urgent Revolutionary Task*, 1870

We do not want to "wait for the masses to become anarchist before making the revolution," the more so since we are convinced that they will never become anarchist if the institutions that keep them enslaved are not first violently destroyed. And since we need the support of the masses to build up a force of sufficient strength to achieve our specific task of radical change of the social organism by the direct action of the masses, we must get closer to them, accept them as they are, and from within their ranks seek to "push" them forward as much as possible. That is, of course, if we really intend to work for the practical achievement of our ideals and are not content with preaching in the desert for the simple satisfaction of our intellectual pride.

ERRICO MALATESTA, *Umanità Nova*, November 25, 1922

The International does not have and never will have any other power but the great power of opinion, and it will never be anything else but the organization of the natural action of the individuals upon the masses. In contrast, the State and all its institutions—the Church, the University, the courts, financial science, the police, and the Army—demand the passive obedience of their subjects.

MICHAEL BAKUNIN, *Protestation of the Alliance*, 1871

The task of the conscious minority is to profit from every situation to change the environment in a way that will make the education and spiritual elevation of the people possible, without which there is no real way out.

ERRICO MALATESTA, *Umanità Nova,* September 30, 1920

First of all, the insurrection must proceed among the peasantry and urban workers themselves. Only then can it count on success. But no less necessary for the success of the insurrection is the existence among the insurrectionists themselves of a strong, friendly, active group of people who, serving as a bond between the separate localities and having clearly determined how to formulate the demands of the people, how to avoid various traps, how to secure its victory, are agreed on the means of action. It is clear, moreover, that such a party must not stand outside the people but among them, must serve, not as a champion of some alien opinions worked out in isolation, but as a more distinct, more complete expression of the demands of the people themselves.

PETER KROPOTKIN, *Must We Occupy Ourselves . . . ?* 1873

The masses, in the future revolution, will constitute, in a sense, the infantry of the revolutionary army. Our Anarchist groups, specialized in technical needs, will form, so to speak, the artillery, which, though less numerous, is no less necessary than the infantry.

SIEGFRIED NACHT, speech at the Congress of the Anarchist International, Amsterdam, 1907

The social revolution can only be the work of the masses. But all revolutions must be necessarily accompanied by acts that, by their character—technical in some ways—can only be the deed of a small number, the hardiest and most trained fraction of the proletariat in motion. In each neighborhood, each city, each region, our groups will form, in the revolutionary period, so many little combat organizations, each destined to accomplish the special and delicate measures that the great mass is often incapable of.

AMADÉE DUNOIS, speech at the Congress of the
Anarchist International, Amsterdam, 1907

The masses will make the insurrection but cannot prepare it technically. Men, groups, and parties are needed who are joined by free agreement, under oath of secrecy, and provided with the necessary means to create a network of speedy communications to keep those concerned informed of all incidents likely to provoke a widespread popular movement.

ERRICO MALATESTA, *Umanità Nova,* August 7, 1920

But, you will say, to start a revolution and bring it to its conclusion one needs a force that is . . . armed. And who denies this? This armed force, or rather the numerous armed revolutionary groups, will be performing a revolutionary task if they serve to free the people and prevent the re-emergence of an authoritarian government. But they will be tools of reaction and destroy their own achievements if they are prepared to be used to impose a particular kind of social organization or the program of a particular party.

ERRICO MALATESTA, *Fede!,* November 25, 1923

The Socialist aim . . . consists in making every worker fully conscious of what he wants by awakening in him an intelligence that corresponds to his instinct, for when the intelligence of workers rises to the level of their instinct, their will crystallizes and their might becomes irresistible.

MICHAEL BAKUNIN, *The Politics of the International,* 1869

Everything depends on what the people are capable of wanting. In past insurrections the people, unaware of the real reasons for their misery, have always wanted very little and have achieved very little. What will they want from the next insurrection?

The answer, in part, depends on our propaganda and the effort we put into it.

ERRICO MALATESTA, *Il Programma Anarchico,* 1920

Instinct, left to itself and not yet transformed into conscious, clearly defined thought, is easily misled, perverted, and deceived. And it is impossible for it to rise to self-awareness without the aid of education, of science—the knowledge of affairs and of men—and of political experience. All this is lacking so far as the proletariat is concerned.

MICHAEL BAKUNIN, *The Knouto-Germanic Empire,* 1871

What do the masses lack to be able to overthrow the prevailing social order so detestable to them? They lack two things—organization and science—precisely the two things that constitute now, and always have constituted, the power of governments.

MICHAEL BAKUNIN, *Protestation of the Alliance,* 1871

It is evident that during the preparatory period that we are going through today, we must concentrate all our efforts on propagandizing the idea of expropriation and collectivism. Instead of relegating these principles to a corner of our brain, so as to speak to people only of so-called politics (which would prepare their minds for a revolution eminently political, perceptibly obliterating its economic character, the only thing that can give it the necessary force), we must, to the contrary, always and in all circumstances, expose these principles, demonstrating the practical implication, proving the necessity; we must make all efforts to prepare the popular mind to accept these ideas.

PETER KROPOTKIN, Report to the Jura Workers' Federation, 1879

To imagine that a government can be overturned by a secret society, and that that secret society can take its place, is an error common to all the revolutionary organizations that sprang to life in the bosom of the republican middle class since 1820. And yet facts abound that prove what an error it is. . . .

. . . For it is not secret societies nor even revolutionary organizations that can give the finishing blow to governments. Their function, their historic mission, is to prepare men's minds for the revolution, and then when men's minds are prepared and external circumstances are favorable, the final rush is made, not by the group that initiated the movement, but by the mass of the people altogether outside of the [secret] society.

PETER KROPOTKIN, *Revolutionary Government,* 1880

What matters most of all is that the people, all people, should lose the sheeplike instincts and habits with which their minds have been inculcated by an agelong slavery, and that they should learn to think and act freely. It is to this great task of spiritual liberation that anarchists must especially devote their attention.

ERRICO MALATESTA, *Il Risveglio,* December 14, 1929

No handful of people, however energetic and talented, can evoke a popular insurrection, if the people themselves, through their own best representatives, do not achieve the realization that they have no other way out of a position with which they are dissatisfied except insurrection. Consequently, the business of any revolutionary party is not to call for insurrection but only to pave the way for the success of the imminent insurrection—that is, to unite the dissatisfied elements, to promote the acquaintance of separate units or groups with the aspirations and actions of other similar groups, to help the people define more clearly the true causes of dissatisfaction, to help them define more clearly their actual enemies, removing the mask from those enemies who hide behind some decorous disguise, and finally, to contribute to the elucidation of the nearest practical goals and the means of their realization.

PETER KROPOTKIN, *Must We Occupy Ourselves . . . ?* 1873

The social revolution is not a mere political change: it is a fundamental economic, ethical, and cultural transformation. A conspirative minority or political party undertaking such a work must meet with the active and passive opposition of the great majority and therefore degenerate into a system of dictatorship and tyranny.

ALEXANDER BERKMAN, *What Is Communist Anarchism?* 1928

Once such a great natural phenomenon [as a revolution] has begun, . . . separate individuals are powerless to exercise any kind of influence on the course of events. A party perhaps can do something—far less than is usually thought—and on the surface of the oncoming waves, its influence may, perhaps, be very slightly noticeable. But separate small aggregations not forming a fairly large mass are undoubtedly powerless—their powers are *nil* . . . .

PETER KROPOTKIN, letter to the workers of Western Europe, April, 1919

Isolated, sporadic propaganda, which is often a way of easing a troubled conscience or simply an outlet for someone who has a passion for argument, serves little or no purpose. Such propaganda is forgotten and lost before it can have an effect.

What is needed is continuity of effort, patience, coordination, and adaptability to different surroundings and circumstances.

ERRICO MALATESTA, *l'Agitazione,* September 22, 1901

In the next revolution, those who think most quickly to set an example, those who have the most enthusiasm, the most forcefulness, the most vitality, the most élan—it is those whom the crowd will follow.

JEAN GRAVE, *Anarchy, Its Goal, Its Means,* 1899

Mediocrity of thought destroys noble efforts, grand passions, and immense devotions.

PETER KROPOTKIN, *Revolutionary Studies,* 1892

If for the life of the [trade union] organization and for the needs and wishes of its members it is absolutely necessary to negotiate, to compromise, and to establish doubtful contacts with the authorities, so be it; but this must be done by others, not by anarchists, whose role is that of pointing to the insufficiency and precariousness of all improvements that can be obtained under a capitalist regime, and of pushing the struggle always toward more radical solutions.

ERRICO MALATESTA, *Pensiero e Volontà,* April 16, 1925

General rule: The anarchist who accepts the role of a permanent and paid functionary of a union is lost for propaganda, lost for anarchism! He becomes henceforth obliged to those who pay him and, as these are not anarchists, the paid functionary, forced to choose between his conscience and his interest, either will follow his conscience and lose his job, or follow his interest and then, good-bye anarchism!

ERRICO MALATESTA, speech at the Congress of the
Anarchist International, Amsterdam, 1907

We can have relations of cooperation with non-anarchist parties so long as we share a need to fight a common enemy and are unable to destroy him unaided, but as soon as a party takes power and becomes the government, the only relations we can have with it are those between enemies.

ERRICO MALATESTA, *Pensiero e Volontà,*
August 1, 1926

[After the revolution] anarchists will have the special mission of being the vigilant custodians of freedom, against all aspirants to power and against the possible tyranny of the majority.

ERRICO MALATESTA, *Il Risveglio,* December 14, 1929

We must, in every way possible, and in accord with local conditions and possibilities, encourage action by workers' associations, cooperatives, groups of volunteers—in order to prevent the emergence of new authoritarian groups, new governments, combating them with violence if necessary but, above all, by rendering them useless.

ERRICO MALATESTA, *Il Risveglio,* December 14, 1929

In all circumstances, it is the duty of the Socialists, and especially of the Anarchists, to do everything that can weaken the State and the capitalist class, and to take as the only guide to their conduct the interests of Socialism; or, if they are materially powerless to act efficaciously for their own cause, at least to refuse any voluntary help to the cause of the enemy, and stand aside to save at least their principles—which means to save the future.

ERRICO MALATESTA, *Anarchists Have Forgotten
Their Principles,* 1914

We are reformers today in so far as we seek to create the most favorable conditions and a large body of enlightened militants so that an insurrection by the people would be brought to a satisfactory conclusion. We shall be reformers tomorrow, after a triumphant insurrection and the achievement of freedom, in that we will seek with all means that freedom permits—that is, by propaganda, example, and even violent resistance against anyone who would wish to restrict our freedom—to win over to our ideas an ever greater number of people.

But we will never recognize the institutions; we will take or win all possible reforms with the same spirit that one tears occupied territory from the enemy's grasp in order to go on advancing, and we will always remain enemies of every government, whether it be that of the monarchy today or the republican or bolshevik governments of tomorrow.

ERRICO MALATESTA, *Pensiero e Volontà,* March 1, 1924

THE ANARCHIST GROUPS

Organization, action in common, is indispensable to the development of anarchism and it does not contradict our theoretical premises. Organization is a means, and not a principle; but it is self-evident that, to be acceptable, organization must be constituted in a libertarian manner.

GEORGES THOMAR, speech at the Congress of the Anarchist International, Amsterdam, 1907

Anyone who tells you that anarchists don't believe in organization is talking nonsense. Organization is everything, and everything is organized . . .

But there is organization and organization. Capitalist society is so badly organized that its various members suffer . . .

There is organization that is painful because it is ill, and organization that is joyous because it means health and strength . . . the organization built on compulsion, which coerces and forces, is bad and unhealthy. The libertarian organization, formed voluntarily and in which every member is free and equal, is a sound body and can work well. It is the kind of organization the anarchists believe in.

ALEXANDER BERKMAN, *What Is Communist Anarchism?* 1928

With anarchy, he who knows teaches to those who do not know; he who is the first to conceive of a thing puts it into practice while explaining it to those he wants to enlist, but there is no temporary abdication, no authority, there is nothing but equals in mutual aid, according to their respective talents, abandoning nothing of their rights, nothing of their autonomy. The surest means of making anarchy triumph is to act as an anarchist.

JEAN GRAVE, *Dying Society and Anarchy,* 1893

We are sworn enemies of all domination, be it collective or be it individual. . . . We do not want any leaders and we will not tolerate any. An idea, even coming from an individual, if it is a good idea and is accepted, immediately becomes collective property, in order that our ideas will not carry personal labels. That is our custom, our law.

MICHAEL BAKUNIN, letter to Lodovico Nabruzzi,
January 3, 1872

An anarchist organization must [allow for] complete autonomy, and independence, and therefore full responsibility, for individuals and groups; free agreement between those who think it useful to come together for cooperative action, for common aims; a moral duty to fulfill one's pledges and to take no action contrary to the accepted program. On such bases then one then introduces practical forms and suitable instruments to give real life to the organization. Thus the groups, the federation of groups, the federations of federations, meetings, congresses, correspondence committees and so on. But all this must be done freely, in such a way as not to restrict the thought and the initiative of individual members, but only to give greater scope to the efforts which in isolation would be impossible or ineffective.

ERRICO MALATESTA, *Il Risveglio,* October 15, 1927

At present, in revolutionary action as in work, the collective is to replace individuals. You should know that when you are organized you are stronger than all the Mazzinis and Garibaldis in the world. You will think, live, and act collectively, which, however, will in no way hinder the full development of the intellectual and moral faculties of every individual. Every one of you will contribute his own abilities, and in uniting you increase your value a hundred-fold. Such is the law of collective action.

MICHAEL BAKUNIN, *A Circular Letter to My Friends in Italy*, 1871

There are matters in which it is worth accepting the will of the majority because the damage caused by a split would be greater than that caused by the error; there are circumstances in which discipline becomes a duty, because to fail in it would be to fail in the solidarity among the oppressed and would mean betrayal in the face of the enemy. But when one is convinced that the organization is pursuing a wrong course, which threatens the future and makes it difficult to remedy the harm done, then there is a duty to rebel and to resist even at the risk of provoking a split.

ERRICO MALATESTA, *Pensiero e Volontà*, February 16, 1925

For the State, centralism is the appropriate form of organization, since it aims at the greatest possible uniformity in social life for the maintenance of political and social equilibrium. But for a movement whose very existence depends on prompt action at any favorable moment and on the independent thought and action of its supporters, centralism could but be a curse, by weakening its power of decision and systematically repressing all immediate action.

RUDOLF ROCKER, *Anarcho-Syndicalism*, 1938

We must not let the enemies of the people believe that we take one or the other of us for idols.

LOUISE MICHEL, speech, 1881 (?)

We follow ideas, not men, and rebel at this habit of embodying a principle in a man.

ERRICO MALATESTA, speech at the Berne
Congress of the International, 1876

It is the leader who must think for all; it is the leader who is charged with the duty of watching for the well-being and liberty of the mass in general and the individual in particular; the result being that there are millions of brains among the mass that never think. . . . The masses remain passive. . . .

There should be no mass; there should be a league of thinking individualities, united among themselves for the attainment of certain ends.

RICARDO FLORES MAGON, *Anarchist Revolutionary
Almanack,* 1914

The International Workingmen's Association can become an instrument of the emancipation of humanity only when it has first emancipated itself, and that will happen only when it has ceased dividing into two groups—the majority as blind tools, and the minority of learned savants who do all the directing—and when every member of the Association has become imbued with the science, philosophy, and politics of Socialism.

MICHAEL BAKUNIN, *Protestation of the Alliance,* 1871

At the moment of action, in the midst of struggle, roles are naturally distributed in accordance with everyone's aptitudes and judged by the whole collective; some direct and command while others execute commands. But no function remains fixed and petrified, nothing is irrevocably attached to one person. Hierarchic order and advancement do not exist, so that the executive of yesterday may become the subordinate of today. . . .

In such a system, power, properly speaking, no longer

exists. Power is diffused in the collective and becomes the sincere expression of the liberty of everyone. . . .

This is the only true human discipline.

MICHAEL BAKUNIN, *The Knouto-Germanic Empire,* 1871

I believe, as I have always believed, in liberty. Liberty understood in the sense of responsibility. I consider discipline indispensable, but it must be self-discipline moved by a common ideal and a strong feeling of comradeship . . .

For me, discipline has no other significance than the concept one has of responsibility. I am the enemy of the discipline of the barracks, which leads to brutality, to horror, and to mechanical action . . . and which is the refuge of cowards. In our organization, . . . the members accept and carry out the decisions made by the committees, which are proposed by comrades elected to discharge these responsibilities. . . . If we know that we are opposed by hesitant ones, then let us speak to their consciousness and to their self-esteem. In this manner, we would make them good comrades.

BUENAVENTURA DURRUTI, interview with Emma Goldman, 1936

In order to establish a certain coordination in action, one which, in my opinion, is necessary among serious people striving toward the same goal, certain conditions are required: a definite set of rules equally binding upon all, certain agreements and understandings to be frequently renewed. Lacking all that, if everyone is to work as he pleases, even the most serious people will find themselves in a position whereby they neutralize one another's efforts.

MICHAEL BAKUNIN, *The Printed Word and Revolution,* n.d.

The army of Makhnovist rebels was organized on the basis of three fundamental principles: voluntary service, election of officers, and self-discipline.

Voluntary service signifies that the army was composed only of revolutionary combatants entering it of their own free will.

The election of officers means that the commanders of all the parts of the army, the members of the general staff and of the council, and thus all the persons occupying important posts in the army had to be elected or accepted by the rebels of the different units or by the whole of the army.

Self-discipline signifies that all the rules of discipline of the army were drawn up by committees of rebels, then validated by general meetings, and were rigorously observed under the responsibility of each rebel and each commander.

PETER ARSHINOV, *History of the Makhnovist Movement,* 1928

The soldier of the revolution will not fight effectively if he is converted into a machine without a soul under the rigid discipline of a code that never speaks of right or duty, but only of obedience and punishment. The old formulas are unacceptable, because they were not dictated by a people defending themselves.

Proclamation of the CNT (National Confederation of Labor of Spain), 1936

We want to be the militia of liberty, but not soldiers under uniform. Armies prove dangerous to the people; except for the popular militia protecting the public liberties. Militia, yes! Soldiers, never!

Proclamation of the CNT, 1936

"THIS IS OUR CAREER AND OUR TRIUMPH"

There is a general rule to the effect that those who want to spread the revolution by means of propaganda must be revolutionists themselves. One must have the devil within him in order to be able to rouse the masses; otherwise, there can be only abortive speeches and empty clamor, but not revolutionary acts.

MICHAEL BAKUNIN, *The Knouto-Germanic Empire*, 1871

[The revolutionist] must have within himself the revolutionary passion; he must love liberty and justice to the point of wanting to contribute to their triumph by his efforts, to the point of making it his duty to sacrifice for them his rest, his well-being, his vanity, his personal ambition, and also often his personal interests.

MICHAEL BAKUNIN, *The Program of the Fraternity*, 1865

One who casts his lot with an advanced party must be prepared to spend a number of years in prison, and he need not grudge it. He feels that even during his imprisonment he remains not quite an inactive part of the movement which spreads and strengthens the ideas that are dear to him.

PETER KROPOTKIN, *Memoirs of a Revolutionist*, 1899

I might have live out my life talking at street corners to scorning men. I might have die, unmarked, unknown, a failure. Now we are not a failure. This is our career and our triumph. Never in our full life could we hope to do such work for tolerance, for justice, for man's understanding of man as now we do by accident. Our words—our lives—our pains—nothing! The taking of our lives—lives of a good shoemaker and a poor fish-peddler—all! That last moment belongs to us—that agony is our triumph.

BARTOLOMEO VANZETTI, statement after being sentenced to death along with Nicola Sacco, 1927

SPIES: There will come a time when our silence will be more powerful than the voices you strangle today!

FISCHER: Hurrah for anarchy—
ENGEL: Hurrah for anarchy!
FISCHER: This is the happiest moment of my life!
PARSONS: Will I be allowed to speak, O men of America?
Let me speak, Sheriff Matson! Let the voice of the people
be heard!

> Chicago anarchists, just before being hanged for
> "conspiracy" in the Haymarket bombing,
> November 11, 1887

All of us, without exception, are obliged to live more or less in contradiction with our ideals; but we are anarchists and socialists because, and insofar as, we suffer by this contradiction and seek to make it as small as possible. In the event of adapting ourselves to the environment, we would of course lose the desire to change it and would become ordinary bourgeois; bourgeois without money, perhaps, but for all that, bourgeois in our actions and intentions.

> ERRICO MALATESTA, *l'Anarchia*, August, 1896

The necessary and primary condition of any success whatsoever among the peasants and the workers is full renunciation of any signs of nobility, the lowering of one's material circumstances almost to the level of the milieu where one intends to act. And one must work, do actual work, which each worker and each peasant can understand precisely as work.

> PETER KROPOTKIN, *Must We Occupy
> Ourselves . . . ?* 1873

Only those whose former way of life, whose previous deeds are wholly of a character that merits the faith of the peasantry and workers will be heeded by them; and this will be only the activists of the peasantry itself and those who will wholeheartedly surrender themselves to the people's affairs and prove themselves, not with heroic deeds in a moment of enthusiasm, but with all their previous ordinary life; those who, having cast off any shade of nobility in life, now enter into close relations with the peasantry and urban workers, tied by personal friendship and confidence. Finally, once the need for unification of the people's awakened forces is recognized, then the conclusion seems unavoidable that the only possible place is among the peasantry and workers themselves. Such a way of life serves as direct proof to one's associates that professed convictions are not simple verbiage but a matter of one's whole life.

PETER KROPOTKIN, *Must We Occupy Ourselves . . . ?* 1873

If a man born and raised in a bourgeois environment wishes sincerely and without phrase-mongering to become a friend and brother of the workers, he must renounce all the conditions of his past existence, all his bourgeois habits, break all ties of feelings, vanity, and mind which bind him to the bourgeois world, and, turning his back on that world, becoming its enemy and declaring ruthless war upon it, plunge completely and unreservedly into the worker's world.

MICHAEL BAKUNIN, *The Knouto-Germanic Empire,* 1871

I shall continue to be an impossible person so long as those who are possible remain possible.

MICHAEL BAKUNIN, letter to Ogarov, June 14, 1868

I cannot enjoy what I am eating if I think that there are people dying of hunger; . . . If I am enjoying myself, my spirit is saddened as soon as I recall that there are unfortunate fellow beings still languishing in jail; if I study, or do a job I enjoy doing, I feel remorse at the thought that there are so many brighter than I who are obliged to waste their lives on exhausting, often useless, or harmful tasks.

Clearly, pure egoism, others call it altruism, call it what

you like. But without it, it is not possible to be real anarchists.

ERRICO MALATESTA, *Umanità Nova*, September 16, 1922

It is often said that anarchists live in a world of dreams to come and do not see the things which happen today. We see them only too well, and in their true colors, and that is what makes us carry the hatchet into the forest of prejudices that besets us.

PETER KROPOTKIN, *Anarchism: Its Philosophy and Ideal*, n.d.

To be an anarchist it is not enough to recognize that anarchism is a beautiful ideal; in theory everyone would agree, including sovereigns, leaders, capitalists, police, and I imagine even Mussolini himself. But one must want to struggle to achieve anarchism, or at least to approximate it, by seeking to reduce the power of the state and of privilege, and by demanding always greater freedom, greater justice.

ERRICO MALATESTA, *Pensiero e Volontà,*
May 16, 1925

To the daring belongs the future.

EMMA GOLDMAN, *The Blast,* January 15, 1916

I despise you. I despise your order; your laws, your force-propped authority. *Hang me for it!*

LOUIS LINGG, on being sentenced to hang, 1886

.

WHO MAKES THE REVOLUTION?

.

If we believe that it is sufficient to overthrow the government, then we will become an army of conspirators, but we . . . do not conceive of the revolution in this way. The next revolution must from its inception bring about the seizure of the entire social wealth by the workers in order to transform it into common property. This revolution can succeed only through the workers, only if the urban and rural workers everywhere carry out this objective themselves. To that end, they must initiate their own action in the period *before the revolution;* this can happen only if there is a strong *workers' organization.* The revolutionary bourgeoisie can overthrow the government but it cannot make the revolution; this only the people can do.

PETER KROPOTKIN, speech at the London
Anarchist Congress, 1881

By the *flower of the proletariat,* I mean, above all, that great mass, those millions of non-civilized, disinherited, wretched illiterates whom Messrs. Engels and Marx mean to subject to the paternal regime of *a very strong government,* to employ an expression used by Engels. . . . Without doubt, this will be for their own salvation, as of course all governments, as is well known, have been established solely in the interests of the masses themselves. By the flower of the proletariat I mean precisely that eternal "meat" for governments, that great *rabble of the people* ordinarily designated by Messrs. Marx and Engels by the phrase, at once picturesque and contemptuous, *lumpenproletariat,* the "riff-raff," that rabble which, being very nearly unpolluted by all bourgeois civilization, carries in its heart, in its aspirations, in all the necessities and miseries of its collective position, all the germs of the Socialism of the future, and which alone is powerful enough today to inaugurate the Social Revolution and bring it to triumph.

MICHAEL BAKUNIN, fragment continuation of
The Knouto-Germanic Empire, 1872

It is the "barbarians" [the proletariat] who now represent faith in human destiny and the future of civilization, whereas the "civilized people" find their salvation only in barbarism: the massacre of the [Paris] Communards and the return to the Pope.

MICHAEL BAKUNIN, *Protestation of the Alliance,* 1871

Armed workers and peasants are the only effective defense of the revolution. By means of their unions and syndicates they must always be on guard against counterrevolutionary attack. The worker in factory and mill, in mine and field, is the soldier of the revolution. He is at his bench and plow or on the battlefield according to need. But in his factory as in his regiment he is the soul of the revolution, and it is *his* will that decides its fate. In industry the shop committees, in the barracks the soldiers' committees—these are the fountainhead of all revolutionary strength and activity.

ALEXANDER BERKMAN, *What Is Communist
Anarchism?* 1928

When a nation of many millions of men rises to defend itself, resolved to destroy all and let itself be exterminated with all its property rather than submit to slavery, there is no army in the world, however scientifically organized, and however well provided with arms of the most extraordinary and novel kinds, that can conquer it.

MICHAEL BAKUNIN, *Letters to a Frenchman,* 1870

THE REVOLUTIONARY LABOR MOVEMENT (ANARCHO-SYNDICALISM)

We realize that the road to reconstruction of the world is not free from obstacles, errors, and crossroads. No human being is infallible . . . no matter how revolutionary or proletarian he may be. What is important as a first step is to create the organism that will have to solve the daily and immediate problems of the Revolution. This organism we believe can be no other than organized labor, without intervention of the State and without intermediaries and parasites.

D. A. DE SANTILLAN, *After the Revolution,* 1936

The syndicalist task has a double object: it must pursue, with indefatigable rigor, the amelioration of the present conditions of the working class. But, without being obsessed by this transitory work, the laborers must work to make possible, and soon, the primordial act of complete emancipation: the expropriation of the capitalists.

EMILE POUGET, *The Syndicate,* 1905

[The] necessary task of revolutionary cohesion will be realized in the bosom of the syndicalist organization: there, a growing minority is constituted and develops, aiming to acquire enough power to at first counterbalance, and later, to annihilate, the forces of exploitation and oppression.

EMILE POUGET, *The Character of Direct Action,* 1908

The International Anarchist Congress regards the labor unions as combat organizations in the class struggle for amelioration of the conditions of work, and as unions of producers able to serve in the transformation of capitalist society to an anarchist communist society.

> CHRISTIAN CORNELISSEN, K. VOHRYZEK, and ERRICO MALATESTA, statement at the Congress of the Anarchist International, Amsterdam, 1907

Anarcho-Syndicalists are convinced that a Socialist economic order cannot be created by the decrees and statutes of a government, but only by the solidaric collaboration of the workers with hand or brain in each special branch of production; that is, through the taking over of the management of all plants by the producers themselves under such form that the separate groups, plants, and branches of industry are independent members of the general economic organism and systematically carry on production and the distribution of the products in the interest of the community on the basis of free mutual agreements.

> RUDOLF ROCKER, *Anarcho-Syndicalism,* 1938

Anarcho-Syndicalists are . . . of the opinion that trade-union organization should be of such character as to afford workers the possibility of achieving the utmost in their struggle against the employers, and at the same time provide them with a basis from which they will be able in a revolutionary situation to proceed with the reshaping of economic and social life.

> RUDOLF ROCKER, *Anarcho-Syndicalism,* 1938

The groups of productive workers must become the growing cells of the new society. It is impossible to conceive of a real social transformation on other bases. It is indispensable, then, that the productive workers prepare themselves for their task of expropriation and of reorganization which they alone are capable of successfully accomplishing.

> EMILE POUGET, *The Syndicate,* 1905

For the Anarcho-Syndicalists, the trade union is by no means a mere transitory phenomenon bound up with the duration of capitalist society; it is the germ of the Socialist economy of the future, the elementary school of Socialism in general. Every new social structure makes organs for itself in the body of the old organism. . . . Even revolutions can only develop and mature the germs which already exist and have made their way into the consciousness of men. . . .

RUDOLF ROCKER, *Anarcho-Syndicalism,* 1938

The "Know thyself" of Socrates is, in the union, completed by the maxim "Do thy affairs thyself!"

EMILE POUGET, *The Syndicate,* 1905

Syndicalism exercises a social action which, without manifesting itself in direct participation in parliamentary life, nevertheless has no less an object than to destroy the modern State, to smash it, to absorb it. Pursuing complete emancipation, it cannot limit itself to liberating the worker from capitalism and leaving him under the yoke of the State.

EMILE POUGET, *The General Confederation of Labor,* 1908

Laboratory of economic struggles, detached from electoral competition, in favor of the general strike with all its consequences, the labor union is then just the organization, simultaneously revolutionary and libertarian, which alone will be able to counterbalance and ultimately reduce the fatal influence of the reformist politicians.

FERNAND PELLOUTIER, *Anarchism and the Workers' Unions,* 1895

Just as there is only one working class, there can be, in each trade and in each city, only one workers' organization, only one trade union. On this condition alone, the class struggle—no longer shackled at all times by the squabbling of rival schools and sects—will be able to develop fully and to maximum effect.

PIERRE MONATTE, speech at the Congress of the
Anarchist International, Amsterdam, 1907

Certainly the social problem cannot be solved by wage struggles alone, but they are the best educative instrument for making the workers acquainted with the real essence of the social problem, training them for the struggle for liberation from economic and social slavery.

RUDOLF ROCKER, *Anarcho-Syndicalism*, 1938

The strength of labor is not on the field of battle. It is in the shop, in the mine and factory. There lies its power, that no army in the world can defeat, no human agency conquer.

In other words, the social revolution can take place only by means of the *General Strike*. The General Strike, rightly understood and thoroughly carried out, *is* the social revolution . . . . You can shoot people to death, but you can't shoot them to work.

ALEXANDER BERKMAN, *What Is Communist
Anarchism?* 1928

For the workers, the general strike takes the place of the barricades of the political uprising. It is for them a logical outcome of the industrial system whose victims they are today, and at the same time it offers them their strongest weapon in their struggle for liberation, provided [that] they recognize their own strength and learn how to use this weapon properly.

RUDOLF ROCKER, *Anarcho-Syndicalism*, 1938

The general strike has always appeared to me as an excellent means of opening the social revolution. At the same time, let us be very careful not to fall into the fatal illusion that, with the general strike, armed insurrection becomes a redundancy.

ERRICO MALATESTA, speech at the Congress of the
Anarchist International, Amsterdam, 1907

The anarchists consider the syndicalist movement and the general strike as powerful revolutionary means, but not as substitutes for the Revolution.

International Anarchist Congress, 1907

Since economic slavery is the product of political servitude, to eliminate one it is necessary to eliminate the other, even if Marx said otherwise.

Why does the peasant bring corn to the boss?

Because the gendarme is there to oblige him to do so.

Thus, trade unionism cannot be an end in itself; the struggle must also be waged at a political level so as to identify the role of the State.

ERRICO MALATESTA, *Umanità Nova*, March 14, 1922

Anarchists must recognize the importance of the workers' movement, must favor its development and make it a lever for their action, doing all they can so that, in conjunction with all existing progressive forces, it will culminate in a social revolution leading to the suppression of classes and to complete freedom, equality, peace, and solidarity among all human beings. But it would be a great and fatal illusion to believe, as many do, that the workers' movement can and must on its own, by its very nature, lead to such a revolution. On the contrary, all movements founded in material and immediate interests (and a mass working-class movement cannot be founded in anything else), lacking the ferment, the drive, and the unremitting efforts of men of ideas struggling and making sacrifices for an ideal future, tend to adapt themselves to circumstances, to foster a conservative spirit and the fear of change in those who manage to improve their conditions, and often end by creating new privileged classes and serving to support and consolidate the system that one would want to destroy.

Hence the impelling need for strictly anarchist organizations which struggle both inside and outside the trade unions for the achievement of anarchism and which seek to sterilize all the germs of degeneration and reaction.

ERRICO MALATESTA, *Il Risveglio,* October 15, 1927

Skilled workers [in the United States] look down on manual workers; whites despise and oppress blacks; the "real Americans" consider the Chinese, Italians, and other foreign workers as inferiors. If a revolution were to come in the United States, the strong and wealthy unions would inevitably be against the movement, because they would be worried about their investments and the privileged position they have assured for themselves.

ERRICO MALATESTA, *Umanità Nova,* April 13, 1922

In normal times, when there is no faith in an imminent revolution, just try to persuade workers at the Arsenals who are threatened with unemployment not to demand that the government should build new battleships! . . . All this, and much more that could be said, shows that the workers' movement in itself, without the ferment of revolutionary imagination contrasting with the short-term interests of the workers, without the criticism and impulse of the revolutionaries, far from leading to the transformation of society to the advantage of all, tends to encourage group egoism and to create a class of privileged workers living on the backs of the great mass of the "disinherited."

ERRICO MALATESTA, *Umanità Nova,* April 6, 1922

The structure of existing workers' organizations corresponds to present-day conditions of economic life, which are the result of historical developments and capitalist domination. The new society cannot be achieved without breaking

up those structures and creating new organisms corresponding to the new conditions and the new social objectives.

. . . Of what use, just to quote one of a thousand exam-
ples that come to mind, will be the organizations of the
marble quarrymen of Carrara when what will be needed is
that they should go and cultivate the land and increase the
production of foodstuffs, leaving to the future the construction of monuments and marble palaces.

ERRICO MALATESTA, *Umanità Nova,* April 6, 1922

Every fusion or confusion between the anarchist movement and the trade-union movement ends either by rendering the latter unable to carry out its specific task or by
weakening, distorting, or extinguishing the anarchist spirit.

ERRICO MALATESTA, *Pensiero e Volontà,* April 16, 1925

I am far from hostile to trade unionism, above all when its
tendencies are toward the revolution. But ultimately the
workers' organization is not anarchist, and in consequence
. . . our activity there will never be wholly anarchist. Hence
we must create libertation groups and federations, founded
on respect for liberty and the initiative of all and of each.

GEORGES THONAR, speech at the Congress of the
Anarchist International, Amsterdam, 1907

PEASANTS AND FARM WORKERS

Why, after so many superhuman efforts, after so many
revolutions that are at first always victorious, after so many
painful sacrifices and so many fights for liberty, why does
Europe yet remain enslaved? Because in all the countries of
Europe there is still an immobile mass, at least in appearance, which has remained until now inaccessible to the ideas
of emancipation, humanity, and justice—the mass of peasants. It is that which today constitutes the power, the last
support, and the last refuge of all the despots, a real club in

their hands to crush us. As long as we have not penetrated that mass with our aspirations, our passions, our ideas, we will not cease to be slaves. We must emancipate it in order to emancipate ourselves.

MICHAEL BAKUNIN, *The International and Mazzini,* 1871

In order for the peasants to rise up, it is absolutely necessary that the initiative in this revolutionary movement be taken by city workers, for it is they who combine in themselves the instincts, ideas, and conscious will of the Social Revolution.

MICHAEL BAKUNIN, *Letters to a Frenchman,* 1870

It is true that the revolution first breaks out in industrial rather than in agricultural localities. This is natural since these are greater centers of laboring population and therefore also of popular dissatisfaction. But if the industrial proletariat is the *avant-garde* of revolution, the farm laborer is its backbone. If the latter is weak or broken, the *avant-garde,* the revolution itself, is lost.

ALEXANDER BERKMAN, *What Is Communist Anarchism?* 1928

Since revolution cannot be *imposed* upon the villages, *it must be generated right there, by promoting a revolutionary movement among the peasants themselves, leading them on to destroy through their own efforts the public order, all the political and civil institutions, and to establish and organize anarchy in the villages.*

MICHAEL BAKUNIN, *Letters to a Frenchman,* 1870

In the interests of the revolution, the workers should stop flaunting their disdain for the peasants. In the face of the bourgeois exploiter, the worker should feel that he is the brother of the peasant.

MICHAEL BAKUNIN, *Letters to a Frenchman,* 1870

There remains the question of peasant proprietors. Should they refuse to join forces with the others, there would be no reason to harass them so long as they do the work themselves and do not exploit the labor of others. . . . The disadvantages, the virtual impossibility, of isolated work would soon attract them into the orbit of the collectivity.

ERRICO MALATESTA, *Umanità Nova,* May 15, 1920

It is absolutely necessary that the next revolution not be limited to the big cities: The uprising for expropriation must be generated, above all, in the countryside. Without counting on the revolutionary *élan* that could, in a period of effervescence, radiate from the cities to the villages—we must begin today to lay the groundwork in the countryside.

PETER KROPOTKIN, Report to the Jura Workers' Federation, 1879

EDUCATED YOUTH AND
THE INTELLECTUAL PROLETARIAT

[The revolutionary] must understand that such a complete and radical transformation of society must necessarily involve the destruction of all privileges, all monopolies, all constituted powers, and that this naturally cannot be affected by peaceful means; that, for the same reason, revolutionary transformation will have against it all the powerful, all the rich, and for it, in all countries, only the people, and also that intelligent and truly noble part of the youth who, though belonging by birth to the privileged, by their generous convictions and ardent aspirations, embrace the cause of the people.

MICHAEL BAKUNIN, *The Program of the Fraternity,* 1865

The world of educated, reckless youngsters, not finding a place for themselves or an opportunity for occupation in

Russia—this is the phalanx of thousands which, consciously or unconsciously, belongs to the revolution.

MICHAEL BAKUNIN, correspondence, n.d.

From now on, it is necessary that this youth be present, not as a witness but as an active participant in the front rank of action, and that it must be ready to sacrifice itself, in all places and at all times, in all the popular movements and uprisings, the biggest as well as the smallest . . . It is necessary that, by acting in accordance with a rigorously conceived and efficacious plan and by submitting in this sense to the strictest discipline, in order to create that unanimity without which no victory is possible, it teach itself and teach the people not only to resist wildly, but also to pass boldly to the attack.

MICHAEL BAKUNIN, *Statism and Anarchy*, 1873

Generally speaking, any propagandizing among the educated youth requires so much erudition and dialectics that it involves a terribly unproductive waste of time and a distraction of energy from incomparably more urgent matters. Moreover, those of the young who sincerely seek a way out of their doubts will, on finding out the necessary facts, inevitably come to the same conclusion themselves concerning the need for revolutionary activity.

PETER KROPOTKIN, *Must We Occupy Ourselves . . . ?* 1873

What can our intellectual proletariat do, the Russian socialist-revolutionary youth, upright, sincere, and devoted to the extreme? It must indubitably go to the people, because today, all over the world, but above all in Russia, outside of the people, outside of the millions and millions of proletarians, there is neither existence, nor cause, nor future.

MICHAEL BAKUNIN, *Statism and Anarchy*, 1873

The class that we call our intellectual proletariat and that in Russia is already in a frankly sociorevolutionary situation —in other words, in an impossible and desperate situation— must now be imbued with a passion founded on reason for the socialist-revolutionary cause, if it does not want to succumb shamefully to total ruin; it is this class that henceforth is called to be the organizer of the popular revolution. . . . Certainly, this class, thanks to the instruction it has received, would have been able to find a more or less advantageous little place in the already well-filled and not very cordial ranks of the robbers, exploiters, and oppressors of the people. But . . . these places are more and more rare, so much so that they are accessible only to a very few. Most of the beneficiaries, besides, will reap only the shame of treason and end their life in need, emptiness, and baseness. Our appeal is addressed, then, only to those for whom treason is inconceivable, indeed impossible.

MICHAEL BAKUNIN, *Statism and Anarchy*, 1873

Some hundreds of young people with good intentions are, of course, insufficient to organize a revolutionary force apart from the people. . . . But these hundreds are enough to organize a revolutionary force from among the people.

MICHAEL BAKUNIN, writings on Russia, n.d.

ANARCHY

·

"FREEDOM IS . . . THE POSSIBILITY OF ACTING"

I am a fanatic lover of liberty, regarding it as the unique condition under which intelligence, dignity, and the happiness of men can develop and grow; not that purely formal liberty, conceded, measured, and regulated by the State, an eternal lie that in reality never represents anything but the privilege of the few founded on the slavery of everyone; not that individualistic, egoist, shabby, and fictional liberty extolled by the school of J.-J. Rousseau and thus by all the other schools of bourgeois liberty, which considers the so-called right of everybody, represented by the State, as the limitation of the right of each, which necessarily and always results in the reduction of the right of each to zero.

No, I mean the only liberty that is truly worthy of the name, the liberty that consists in the full development of all the powers, material, intellectual, and moral, that are latent in everyone; liberty that recognizes no restrictions other than those outlined for us by the laws of our own individual nature; so that, properly speaking, there are no restrictions, since the laws are not imposed on us by some outside legislator. . . .

I mean that liberty of each individual which, far from halting as at a boundary before the liberty of others, finds there its confirmation and its extension to infinity; the illimitable liberty of each through the liberty of all, liberty by solidarity, liberty in equality, liberty triumphing over brute force and the principle of authority which was never anything but the intellectualized expression of that force, liberty which, after having overthrown all heavenly and earthly idols, will found and organize a new world, that of human solidarity, on the ruins of all churches and all States.

MICHAEL BAKUNIN, *The Paris Commune and the*
Notion of the State, 1871

The liberty of man consists solely in this: that he obeys natural laws because he has *himself* recognized them as such, and not because they have been externally imposed upon him by any extrinsic will whatever, divine or human, collective or individual.

MICHAEL BAKUNIN, *God and the State,* 1871

Social solidarity is the first human law; freedom is the second law. Both laws interlink with each other and, being inseparable, constitute the essence of humanity. Thus, freedom is not the negation of solidarity; on the contrary, it represents the development and, so to speak, the humanizing of it.

MICHAEL BAKUNIN, *Program of the Alliance,* 1871

The slavery of a single man on earth, being an offense against even the principle of humanity, is a negation of the liberty of all.

MICHAEL BAKUNIN, *Revolutionary Catechism,* 1865

I am free only when all human beings around me—men and women alike—are equally free. The freedom of others,

far from limiting or negating my liberty, is on the contrary
its necessary condition and confirmation.

MICHAEL BAKUNIN, *The Knouto-Germanic
Empire,* 1871

Freedom is not an abstract right but the possibility of acting: this is true among [anarchists] as well as in society as a
whole. And it is by cooperation with his fellows that man
finds the means to express his activity and his power of
initiative.

ERRICO MALATESTA, *l'Agitazione,* June 11, 1897

True liberty is not a mere scrap of paper called "constitution," "legal right," or "law." It is not an abstraction derived
from the nonreality known as "the State." It is not a *negative*
thing of being free *from* something, because with such freedom you may starve to death. Real freedom, true liberty, is
positive: it is freedom *to* something; it is the liberty to be, to
do; in short, the liberty of actual and active opportunity.

EMMA GOLDMAN, *The Place of the Individual
in Society,* 1930's

Freedom is never attained; it must always be striven for.
Consequently its claims have no limit and can neither be
enclosed in a program nor prescribed as a definite rule for
the future. Each generation must face its own problems,
which cannot be forestalled or provided for in advance. The
worst tyranny is that of ideas which have been handed down
to us, allowing no development in ourselves, and trying to
steamroll everything to one flat universal level.

RUDOLF ROCKER, *London Years,* 1956

There is only one dogma, only one law, only one moral
base for men, and that is liberty. To respect the liberty of
your neighbor is duty; to love it, aid it, serve it, is virtue.

MICHAEL BAKUNIN, *Revolutionary Catechism,* 1865

Respect for the freedom of someone else constitutes the highest duty of men. The only virtue is to love this freedom and serve it. This is the basis of all morality, and there is no other basis.

Since freedom is the result and the clearest expression of solidarity—that is, of mutuality of interests—it can be realized only under conditions of equality. Political equality can be based only upon economic and social equality, and justice is precisely the realization of freedom through such equality.

MICHAEL BAKUNIN, *A Member of the International Answers Mazzini,* 1871

A perfect personality . . . is only possible in a state of society where man is free to choose the mode of work, the conditions of work, and the freedom to work. One to whom the making of a table, the building of a house, or the tilling of the soil is what the painting is to the artist and the discovery to the scientist—the result of inspiration, of intense longing and deep interest in work as a creative force. That being the ideal of Anarchy, its economic arrangements must consist of voluntary productive and distributive associations, gradually developing into free communism, as the best means of producing with the least waste of human energy.

EMMA GOLDMAN, *Anarchism,* 1910

True freedom exists only where it is fostered by the spirit of personal responsibility. Responsibility toward one's fellow men is an ethical feeling arising from human associations and having justice for each and all as its basis. Only where this principle is present is society a real community, developing in each of its members that precious urge toward solidarity which is the ethical basis of every healthy human grouping.

RUDOLPH ROCKER, *Nationalism and Culture,* 1933

The essential principle of anarchy is *individual autonomy.*

EMMA GOLDMAN, speech at the Congress of the Anarchist International, Amsterdam, 1907

The Federation of Free Producers and Free Communes

What is to be the form of government in the future? I hear some of my younger readers reply: "Why, how can you ask such a question? You are a republican." "A republican! Yes, but that word specifies nothing. *Res publica,* that is, the public thing. Now, whoever is interested in public affairs—no matter under what form of government—may call himself a republican. Even kings are republicans."—"Well! You are a democrat?"—"No."—"What! You would have a monarchy?"—"No."—"A constitutionalist?"—"God forbid!"—"You are, then, an aristocrat?"—"Not at all."—"You want a mixed government?"—"Still less."—"What are you, then?"—"I am an anarchist."

"Oh! I understand you; you speak satirically. This is a hit at the government."—"By no means. I have just given you my serious and well-considered profession of faith. Although a firm friend of order, I am (in the full force of the term) an anarchist."

P.-J. Proudhon, What Is Property? 1840

No government at all! No Church at all! No State at all! But will that then be absolute anarchy, the complete disorganization of society? Yes, it will be anarchy from the point of view of politics or government. But it will be the organization of order, of justice, of liberty, of equality—that is to say, the organization of human solidarity—from the point of view of economics and society.

Michael Bakunin, The Political
Theology of Mazzini, fragment, 1871

Anarchy is *society organized without authority,* meaning by authority the power to *impose* one's own will, and not the inevitable and beneficial fact that he who has greater understanding of, as well as the ability to carry out, a task succeeds more easily in having his opinion accepted and in acting as a guide on the particular question for those less able than himself.

In our opinion, authority not only is not necessary for social organization but, far from benefitting it, lives on it parasitically, hampers its development, and uses its advantages for the special benefit of a particular class which exploits and oppresses the others.

ERRICO MALATESTA, *l'Agitazione*, June 4, 1897

In place of the present capitalistic economic order, Anarchists would have a free association of all productive forces based upon cooperative labor, which would have as its sole purpose the satisfying of the necessary requirements of every member of society, and would no longer have in view the special interest of privileged minorities within the social union. In place of the present state-organizations with their lifeless machinery of political and bureaucratic institutions, Anarchists desire a federation of free communities which shall be bound to one another by their common economic and social interests and shall arrange their affairs by mutual agreement and free contract.

RUDOLF ROCKER, *Anarcho-Syndicalism*, 1938

The political and economic organization of social life must start, not, as today, from top to bottom and from the center to the circumference, on the principle of unity and forced centralization, but from bottom to top and from the circumference to the center, on the principle of association and free federation.

MICHAEL BAKUNIN, *Revolutionary Catechism*, 1865

A society founded on serfdom is in keeping with absolute monarchy; a society based on the wage system and the exploitation of the masses by the capitalists finds its political expression in parliamentarism. But a free society, regaining possession of the common inheritance, must seek in free groups and the free federation of groups a new organization, in harmony with the new economic phase of history.

PETER KROPOTKIN, *The Conquest of Bread*, 1892

The Anarchists conceive a society in which all the mutual relations of its members are regulated, not by laws, not by authorities, whether self-imposed or elected, but by mutual agreements between the members of that society, and by a sum of social customs and habits—not petrified by law, routine, or superstition, but continually developing and continually readjusted, in accordance with the ever-growing requirements of a free life, stimulated by the progress of science, invention, and the steady growth of higher ideals.

No ruling authorities, then. No government of man by man; no crystallization and immobility, but a continual evolution—such as we see in nature. Free play for the individual, for the full development of his individual gifts—*for his individualization*.

PETER KROPOTKIN, *Modern Science and Anarchism*, 1913

The idea of independent communes for the territorial organization, and of federations of trade unions for the organization of men in accordance with their different functions, gave a *concrete* conception of society regenerated by a social revolution.

PETER KROPOTKIN, *Modern Science and Anarchism*, 1913

We are guided by the vision of a society of free producers and distributors in which no power exists to take from them the possession of the productive apparatus.

D. A. DE SANTILLAN, *After the Revolution*, 1936

He who with us desires the establishment of freedom, justice, and peace, he who desires the triumph of humanity and the complete liberation of the mass of the people, must desire with us the destruction of all States and the foundation upon their ruins of a world federation of free productive associations in all countries.

MICHAEL BAKUNIN, speech to the League of Peace and Freedom, 1868

As a partisan of liberty, that first condition of humanity, I think that equality must be established in the world by the spontaneous organization of work and of the collective property of the productive associations, freely organized and federalized in communes, and by the equally spontaneous federation of the communes, but not by the supreme and guardian action of the State.

MICHAEL BAKUNIN, *The Paris Commune and the Notion of the State*, 1871

We are struggling for a better and brighter life. Our ideal is to achieve a community of workers, without authority, without parasites, and without commissars.

Our immediate goal is to establish a free soviet regime, without the authority of the bolsheviks, without the pressure of any party whatever.

MAKHNOVITSI, partisan army of the Ukraine, *Appeal to the Red Army*, 1920

In place of the capitalist, private owner, and entrepreneur, after the Revolution we will have factory, shop or industrial councils, constituted of workers, executives, and technicians in representation of the personnel of the enterprise, who will have the right to moderate and recall their delegates. No one knows better than the workers themselves the capacity of each one in [an] . . . establishment. There, where everybody knows everybody, the practice of democracy is possible. The factory council representing all the personnel in a place of work will coordinate the work within that establishment and combine it with similar activities of other establishments or productive groups. . . . No outside factor intervenes. There is complete autonomy.

D. A. DE SANTILLAN, *After the Revolution,* 1936

Every shop and factory should have its special committee to attend to the wants and requirements of the men; not leaders, but members of the rank and file, from the bench and furnace, to look after the demands and complaints of their fellow employees. Such a committee, being on the spot, and constantly under the direction and supervision of the workers, wields no power: it merely carries out instructions. Its members are recalled at will and others selected in their place. . . . It is the workers who decide the matters at issue and carry their decisions out through the shop.

ALEXANDER BERKMAN, *What Is Communist Anarchism?* 1928

The councils of the trade and industrial organizations will take the place of the present government, and this representation of labor will do away, once and forever, with the governments of the past.

EUGENE HINS, Congress of Basel of the First International, 1869

We hasten to add here that we vigorously reject any attempt at social organization which, being alien to the fullest liberty of individuals as well as of associations, would demand the establishment of a regimenting authority, of whatever character it might be.

MICHAEL BAKUNIN, *Federalism, Socialism, and Anti-Theologism,* 1867

The idea of a council system for labor was the practical overthrow of the state as a whole; it stands, therefore, in frank antagonism to any form of dictatorship, which must always have in view the highest development of the power of the state.

RUDOLF ROCKER, *Anarcho-Syndicalism,* 1938

Undoubtedly, economic coordination is necessary, but when it is attained by the State, the remedy is worse than the illness, because it is achieved at the cost of exterminating all the values, initiatives, etc., which have no origin in the State.

D. A. DE SANTILLAN, *After the Revolution,* 1936

Our federal council of the economy is not a political power but an economic and administrative regulating power. It receives its orientation from below and operates in accordance with the resolutions of the regional and national assemblies. It is a liaison corps and nothing else.

D. A. DE SANTILLAN, *After the Revolution,* 1936

Our program [includes] the organization of society through a free federation of workers' associations—industrial and agricultural as well as scientific, artistic, and literary—first into a commune; the federation of communes into regions, of regions into nations, and of nations into a fraternal international union.

MICHAEL BAKUNIN, *A Circular Letter to my Friends in Italy,* October, 1871

The Communes of the next Revolution will not only break down the State and substitute free federation for parliamentary rule: they will depart from parliamentary rule within the Commune itself. They will entrust the free organization of food supply and production to free groups of workers who will federate with like groups in other cities and villages—not through the medium of a communal parliament, but directly, to accomplish their aim.

They will be Anarchist within the Commune as they will be Anarchist outside it—and only thus will they avoid the horrors of defeat, the furies of Reaction.

PETER KROPOTKIN, *The Commune of Paris,* 1891

We are not interested in how the workers, employees, and technicians of a factory will organize themselves. That is their affair. But what is fundamental is that from the first moment of Revolution there should exist a proper cohesion of all the productive and distributive forces. This means that the producers of every locality must come to an understanding with all other localities of the province and country, which must have an international *entente* among the producers of the world.

D. A. DE SANTILLAN, *After the Revolution,* 1936

Through the medium of the local councils of the economy, work attains unity and organization, first on a local basis, second, through the regional council, on a regional basis, and finally, through the federal council of the economy, integrated by delegations from the regional councils, on a national basis.

In all this mechanism of non-capitalist workers' organization, no element . . . of force is inherent.

D. A. DE SANTILLAN, *After the Revolution,* 1936

Shop and factory committees, organized locally, by district, region, and state, and federated nationally, will be the bodies best suited to carry on revolutionary production.

Local and state labor councils, federated nationally, will be the form of organization most adapted to manage distribution by means of the people's cooperatives.

ALEXANDER BERKMAN, *What Is Communist Anarchism?* 1928

For the bourgeois of the Middle Ages, the Commune was an isolated State, clearly separated from others by its borders. For us, "Commune" is no longer a territorial agglomeration; it is rather a generic name, a synonym of the grouping of equals, knowing no borders, no walls. The social Commune will quickly cease to be clearly defined. Each group of the Commune will necessarily be attracted to similar groups of other Communes; they will group together, federate with each other, by bonds at least as solid as those tying them to their fellow townsmen; [they will] constitute a Commune of interests, of which the members will be disseminated through a thousand cities and villages. Each individual will find satisfaction of his needs only in grouping together with other individuals having the same tastes and living in a hundred other Communes.

PETER KROPOTKIN, *Words of a Rebel,* 1885

So as not to fall back into the errors of centralized and bureaucratic administrations, we think that the general interests of the Commune must be administered not by a lone and unique local administration but by different special commissions for each branch of activity, directly constituted by the concerned members of each local service. This procedure would remove the governmental character from the local administrations and would maintain, in its integrity, the principle of autonomy, all while organizing the local interests in the best way.

Workers' Federation of the District of Courtelary, 1880

The federal council of the economy made up of all the nuclei of labor from the simple to the complex, from the bottom up, binds the whole economy of the country and is the result of an infinitely complex system of forces, all converging toward the same end: increased production and better distribution.

D. A. DE SANTILLAN, *After the Revolution,* 1936

For the kingdom of parliamentary orators will be substituted statistical facts, which are infinitely more eloquent and in consonance with the living reality.

D. A. DE SANTILLAN, *After the Revolution,* 1936

The industrial power of the masses, expressed through their libertarian associations—Anarcho-Syndicalism—is alone able to organize successfully the economic life and carry on production. On the other hand, the cooperatives, working in harmony with the industrial bodies, serve as the distributing and exchange media between city and country, and at the same time link in fraternal bond the industrial and agrarian masses. A common tie of mutual service and aid is created which is the strongest bulwark of the revolution—far more effective than compulsory labor, the Red Army, or terrorism. In that way alone can revolution act as a leaven to quicken the development of new social forms and inspire the masses to greater achievements.

EMMA GOLDMAN, *My Disillusionment in Russia*, 1922

The workers themselves must choose their own councils (soviets), which will execute the wishes and orders of these same workers; the councils will then be executive and not have authority. The earth, the factories, the enterprises, the mines, the transportation, etc., the wealth of the people, must belong to the workers who work; they must then be collectivized.

Program-Manifesto of the Makhnovitsi, partisan army of the Ukraine, 1920

Anarchism must be made up of an infinite variety of systems and of individuals free from all fetters. It must be like an experimental field . . . for all types of human temperament.

FREDERICO URALES, *La Anarquía al alcance de todos*, 1930(?)

For anarchy to succeed or simply to advance toward its success, it must be conceived not only as a lighthouse which illuminates and attracts, but as something possible and attainable, not in centuries to come, but in a relatively short time and without relying on miracles.

ERRICO MALATESTA, *Pensiero e Volontà*, 1924

INTERNATIONALISM

The boundaries of the proletarian fatherland have now broadened to the extent of embracing the proletariat of the whole world. This, of course, is just the opposite of the bourgeois fatherland.

MICHAEL BAKUNIN, *Statism and Anarchy,* 1873

Human brotherhood knows no division according to nations and races; it knows only useful workers and harmful exploiters. Against these the working people must fight. . . . Go to the people and suffer with them, inspire the one and strengthen the other in the great fight against the lords of the world, against the oppressors and the exploiters of creative labor!

AARON LIEBERMAN, *Call to the Jewish Youth,* 1876(?)

What, then, is patriotism? "Patriotism, sir, is the last resort of scoundrels," said Dr. Johnson.

EMMA GOLDMAN, *Patriotism,* 1910

Bourgeois patriotism, as I view it, is only a very shabby, very narrow, very mercenary, and deeply antihuman passion, having for its object the preservation and maintenance of the power of the national State—that is, the mainstay of all the privileges of the exploiters throughout the nation.

MICHAEL BAKUNIN, *Letters to a Frenchman,* 1870

[Our organization] recognizes *nationality* as a natural fact, having the incontestable right to exist and develop freely, but it does not recognize it as a *principle*—for every principle should possess the character of universality, whereas nationality, on the contrary, is an exclusive and isolated fact.

MICHAEL BAKUNIN, *Federalism, Socialism, and Anti-Theologism,* 1867

Every nationality, great or small, has the incontestable right to be itself, to live according to its own nature. This right is simply the corollary of the general principle of freedom.

MICHAEL BAKUNIN, *Federalism, Socialism, and Anti-Theologism,* 1867

Will it . . . be necessary, as is sometimes suggested, that the nations in the vanguard of the movement should adapt their pace to those who lag behind? Must we wait till the Communist Revolution is ripe in all civilized countries? Clearly not! Even if it were a thing to be desired, it is not possible. History does not wait for the laggards.

Besides, we do not believe that in any one country the Revolution will be accomplished at a stroke, in the twinkling of an eye, as some socialists dream.

PETER KROPOTKIN, *The Conquest of Bread,* 1892

Against this world reaction the isolated revolution of a single people cannot succeed. It would be a folly . . . on the part of this people and a betrayal of, a crime against, all other peoples. From now on, the insurrection of a people must be carried out, not with regard to that people alone, but to the whole world.

MICHAEL BAKUNIN, *Revolutionary Catechism,* 1865

The expropriation and communizing of social capital must be accomplished everywhere where this deed is possible and as soon as the possibility presents itself, without inquiring whether all or even most of Europe or of other countries is ready to accept the ideas of collectivism. The inconveniences that will result from a partial realization of collectivization will be compensated largely by its advantages. The deed being accomplished in one locality, it will itself become the most powerful means of propaganda and the most powerful motor to activate localities where the worker, little prepared to accept these ideas of collectivism, is hesitant to proceed to expropriation.

PETER KROPOTKIN, report to the Jura
Workers' Federation, 1879

The Revolution cannot be restricted to a single country: it is obliged, on pain of death, to bring along in its movement, if not the entire universe, at least a considerable part . . . .

JAMES GUILLAUME, *Ideas on Social Organisation*, 1876

For one nation to rise up in the interest and in the name of everybody, it must have a program for everyone, large enough, profound enough, in a word, human enough to embrace the interests of everybody and to electrify the passions of all the masses of Europe, regardless of nationality. Such a program can only be that of the democratic and social revolution.

MICHAEL BAKUNIN, *Revolutionary Catechism*, 1865

THE LIBERTARIAN REVOLUTION

For us, the solution of the social problem includes not only the most complete realization possible of material well-being for the benefit of the masses, but also, for all and for each, the complete establishment of liberty.

Worker's Federation of the District of Courtelary, 1880

Whoever believes that freedom of the personality can find a substitute in equality of possessions has not even grasped the essence of socialism. For freedom there is no substitute; there can be no substitute. Equality of economic conditions for each and all is always a necessary precondition for the freedom of man, but never a substitute for it. Whoever transgresses against freedom transgresses against the spirit of socialism. Socialism means the mutual activity of men toward a common goal with equal rights for all. But solidarity rests on free resolve and can never be compelled without changing into tyranny.

RUDOLF ROCKER, *Nationalism and Culture*, 1933

When Lenin—much in the spirit of Mussolini—dared to say that "freedom is a bourgeois prejudice," he only proved that his spirit was quite incapable of rising to socialism, but had remained stuck in the old ideas of Jacobinism. Anyway, it is nonsense to speak of libertarian and authoritarian socialism. Socialism will be free or it will not be at all.

RUDOLF ROCKER, *Nationalism and Culture*, 1933

Of course, if one accepts Lenin's cynical phrase and thinks of freedom as merely a "bourgeois prejudice," then, to be sure, political rights and liberties have no value at all for the workers. But then all the countless struggles of the past, all the revolts and revolutions to which we owe those rights, are also without value. To proclaim this bit of wisdom it would hardly have been necessary to overthrow tsarism, for even the censorship of Nicholas II would certainly have had no objection to the designation of freedom as a "bourgeois prejudice."

RUDOLF ROCKER, *Anarcho-Syndicalism*, 1938

To suppress speech and press is not only a theoretic offense against liberty: it is a direct blow at the very foundations of the revolution.

ALEXANDER BERKMAN, *What Is Communist Anarchism?* 1928

I deny the right of anyone—individually or collectively—to set up an inquisition of thought. Thought is, or should be, free. . . . For the government to attempt to control thought, to prescribe certain opinions or proscribe others, is the height of despotism.

ALEXANDER BERKMAN, declaration to the Department of Immigration Agents, 1919

It is not a question of right or wrong; it is a question of freedom for everybody, freedom for each individual so long as he respects the equal freedom of others.

No one can judge with certainty who is right and who is wrong, who is nearest to the truth, or which is the best way to achieve the greatest good for each and everyone. Freedom coupled with experience is the only way of discovering the truth and what is best; and there can be no freedom if there is denial of the freedom to err.

ERRICO MALATESTA, *Umanità Nova,*
September 11, 1920

Some talk of the right to prevent the dissemination of error. But by what means?

If the strongest current of opinion supports the priests, then it is the priests who will obstruct our propaganda; if, instead, opinion is on our side, what need is there to deny freedom in order to combat an influence on the wane and run the risk that people will feel sympathy for it because it is being persecuted? All other considerations apart, it is in our interest always to be on the side of freedom, because, as a minority proclaiming freedom for all, we would be in a stronger position to demand that others should respect our freedom; and if we are a majority we will have no reason, if we really do not aspire to dominate, to violate the freedom of others. . . . So freedom for everybody and in everything, limited only by equal freedom for others; which does *not* mean—it is almost ridiculous to have to point this out—that we recognize and wish to respect the "freedom" to exploit, to oppress, to command, which is oppression and certainly not freedom.

ERRICO MALATESTA, *La Questione Sociale,*
November 25, 1899

Who . . . is to tell us what is truth and what error? Shall we have to establish a ministry of public education, with its qualified teachers, recognized textbooks, school inspectors, etc.? And all this in the name of the "people," just as with the social democrats, who want to take power in the name of the "proletariat"? . . .

With good reason we say that when the social democrats go to parliament, they virtually cease to be socialists. But this, surely, does not stem from taking a seat in an assembly called parliament; it is the power that goes with the title of member of parliament.

If we, in any way, dominate the lives of others and prevent them from doing what they wish to do, then for all practical purposes we cease to be anarchists.

ERRICO MALATESTA, *La Questione Sociale,*
November 25, 1899

Be it never forgotten that the cure for evil and disorder is *more* liberty, not suppression.

ALEXANDER BERKMAN, *What Is Communist
Anarchism?* 1928

Laws—just laws, natural laws—are not made, they are discovered.

ALBERT PARSONS, on being sentenced to hang, 1886

The FAI [Iberian Anarchist Federation] declares that our revolution must not be the expression of any totalitarian creed but the exponent of all the popular sectors that influence political and social life. As anarchists we are foes of all dictatorships, whether of caste or party; we are enemiés of the totalitarian form of government and believe that the ideals of our people must be the result of the joint action of all sectors that cooperate in building a society without class privileges, in which the organ of administration, work, and coexistence in a federal system must satisfy the needs of all the regions of Spain.

Proclamation of the FAI, Valencia, 1937

We want, first of all, to recognize the right of free experimentation for all social tendencies in our revolution; for this reason, it will not be a new tyranny, but the beginning of a reign of freedom and well-being, in which all forces can express themselves, all initiative be acted on, and all progress be put in practice. Violence is justified in the destruction of the old world of violence, but it is counterrevolutionary and antisocial when it is employed as a reconstructive method.

D. A. DE SANTILLAN, *After the Revolution,* 1936

If in order to win it were necessary to erect the gallows in the public square, then I would prefer to lose.

ERRICO MALATESTA, *Pensiero e Volontà,* 1924

If we do not renounce violence today in order to fight enslaving forces, in the new economic and social order of things we can follow only the line of persuasion and practical experience. We can oppose with force only those who try to subjugate us in behalf of their interests or concepts, but we cannot resort to force against those who do not desire to live as we do. Here, our respect for liberty must encompass the liberty of our adversaries to live their own life, always on condition that they are not aggressive and do not deny freedom to others.

D. A. DE SANTILLAN, *After the Revolution,* 1936

The people do not reign by terror. Invented to forge chains, terror covered by legality forges chains for the people.

PETER KROPOTKIN, *Revolutionary Studies,* 1892

JAILS AND JUSTICE

In the next revolution we hope that this cry will go forth:
"Burn the guillotines; demolish the prisons; drive away the judges, policemen, and informers—the impurest race upon the face of the earth; treat as a brother the man who has been

led by passion to do ill to his fellows; above all, take from the ignoble products of middle-class idleness the possibility of displaying their vices in attractive colors; and be sure that but few crimes will mar our society."

PETER KROPOTKIN, *Law and Authority*, 1886

There is only one answer to the question "What can be done to better this penal system?" Nothing. A prison cannot be improved. With the exception of a few unimportant little improvements, there is absolutely nothing to do but demolish it.

PETER KROPOTKIN, *Prisons and Their Moral Influence on Prisoners*, 1877

How often have prisoners been heard to say: "It's the big thieves who are holding us here; we are the little ones." Who can dispute this when he knows the incredible swindles perpetrated in the realm of high finance and commerce; when he knows that the thirst for riches, acquired by every possible means, is the very essence of bourgeois society; when he has discovered the immense numbers of suspicious transactions between honest men (according to bourgeois standards) and criminals. When he has seen all this, he must be convinced that jails are made for the unskillful, not for criminals.

PETER KROPOTKIN, *Prisons and Their Moral Influence on Prisoners*, 1877

Crime is the necessary condition of the very existence of the State, and it therefore constitutes the State's exclusive monopoly, from which it follows that the individual who dares commit a crime is guilty in a twofold sense: first, he is guilty against human conscience, and, above all, he is guilty against the State in abrogating to himself one of its most precious privileges.

MICHAEL BAKUNIN, *The Bear of Berne and the Bear of St. Petersburg*, 1870

It is true that the professional thief is also a victim of the social environment. The example set by his superiors, his educational background, and the disgusting conditions in which many people are obliged to work easily explain why some men, who are not morally better than their contemporaries, finding themselves with the choice of being exploiters or exploited, choose to be the former. . . . These extenuating circumstances could as well be applied to the capitalists, but in so doing one only demonstrates more clearly the basic identity between the two professions.

ERRICO MALATESTA, *Il Pensiero,* March 16, 1911

Experience teaches us . . . that it is society which always prepares the crime and that the malefactors are only the fatal instruments that accomplish those crimes. It is, then, useless to oppose social immorality with rigorous legislation that usurps individual liberty.

MICHAEL BAKUNIN, *Revolutionary Catechism,* 1865

The theory of culpability and punishment came from theology, that is to say, the marriage of absurdity to religious hypocrisy.

MICHAEL BAKUNIN, *Program and Object of the Secret Revolutionary Organization of International Brothers,* 1868

Experience invariably [shows] that laws, however barbarous they may be, have never served to suppress vice or to discourage delinquency. The more severe the penalties imposed on the consumers and traffickers of cocaine, the greater will be the attraction of forbidden fruits and the fascination of the risks incurred by the consumer, and the greater will be the profits made by the speculators, avid for money.

It is useless, therefore, to hope for anything from the law. We must suggest another solution. Make the use and sale of cocaine free from restrictions and open kiosks where it would be sold at cost price or even under cost. And then launch a great propaganda campaign.

ERRICO MALATESTA, *Umanità Nova,* August 10, 1922

The first duty of the revolution will be to abolish prisons —those monuments of human hypocrisy and cowardice. Antisocial acts need not be feared in a society of equals, among a free people, all of whom have acquired a healthy education and the habit of mutually aiding one another.

PETER KROPOTKIN, *Prisons and Their Moral Influence on Prisoners,* 1877

Libertarian Communism is incompatible with all correctional regimes; it must abolish the existing system of correctional justice and, therefore, the instruments of punishment (jails, penitentiaries, etc.). . . . We consider that:

First—man is not naturally evil, and delinquency is a logical result of the state of social injustice in which we live.

Second—by fulfilling man's needs and by making a rational and humane education available, the causes of crime will disappear.

The Program of the CNT, adopted at Saragossa, May, 1936

The most absurd apology for authority and law is that they serve to diminish crime. Aside from the fact that the State is itself the greatest criminal, breaking every written and natural law, stealing in the form of taxes, killing in the form of war and capital punishment, it has come to an absolute standstill in coping with crime. It has failed utterly to destroy or even minimize the horrible scourge of its own creation.

EMMA GOLDMAN, *Anarchism,* 1910

Fortunately only few men are born or become morally bloodthirsty and sadistic monsters whose death we would not know how to mourn. If these poor devils were to be a continuous threat to everybody and there were no other way of defending ourselves than by killing them, I could also admit the death penalty. But the trouble is that in order to carry out the death penalty one needs an executioner. The executioner is, or becomes, a monster; and on balance it is better to let the monsters that exist go on living rather than to create others.

ERRICO MALATESTA, *Il Risveglio,* February 11, 1933

The number of offenses against existing laws neither increases nor diminishes, *no matter what the system of punishment is.*

PETER KROPOTKIN, *Prisons and Their Moral Influence on Prisoners,* 1877

I would condemn a man who has committed a fault against society to make good the damages.

D. A. DE SANTILLAN, *After the Revolution,* 1936

Human fraternity and liberty are the only correctives to apply to those diseases of the human organism which lead to so-called crime.

PETER KROPOTKIN, *Prisons and Their Moral Influence on Prisoners,* 1877

Our prisons are the reflection of the whole of our life under the present regime; and they will remain what they are now until the whole of our system of government and the whole of our life have undergone a thorough change.

PETER KROPOTKIN, *In Russian and French Prisons,* 1887

Justice must be warm, must be living; it cannot be shut up within the boundaries of a profession. We do not necessarily scorn books and formal procedures but we know for a certainty that there [are] too many lawyers. . . .

Justice is so subtle that all that is needed to interpret it is one's heart.

GARCIA OLIVER, speech in Valencia, January 31, 1937

ANARCHIST ETHICS

We have to create the *new* ethic of the socialist society of the future. *The anarchist working class is creating this ethic.*

PETER KROPOTKIN, letter to Max Nettlau, 1902

Divine morality is based upon two immoral principles: respect for authority and contempt for humanity. Human morality, on the contrary, is based only upon contempt for authority and respect for liberty and humanity.

MICHAEL BAKUNIN, *Integral Education,* 1869

All that was an element of progress in the past or an instrument of moral and intellectual improvement of the human race is due to *the practice of mutual aid,* to the custom that recognized the equality of men and brought them to ally, to unite, to associate. . . .

PETER KROPOTKIN, *Anarchism, Its Philosophy and Ideal,* n.d.

In the practice of mutual aid, which we can retrace to the earliest beginnings of evolution, we thus find the positive and undoubted origin of our ethical conceptions; and we can affirm that in the ethical progress of man, mutual support— not mutual struggle—has had the leading part. In its wide extension, even at the present time, we also see the best guarantee of a still loftier evolution of our race.

PETER KROPOTKIN, *Mutual Aid,* 1902

There are epochs in which the moral conception changes entirely. A man perceives that what he had considered moral is the deepest immorality. In some instances it is a custom, a venerated tradition, that is fundamentally immoral. In others we find a moral system framed in the interests of a single class. We cast them overboard and raise the cry "Down with morality!" It becomes a duty to act "immorally." Let us welcome such epochs. . . . A higher morality has begun to be wrought out.

PETER KROPOTKIN, *Anarchist Morality*, 1909

To make men moral it is necessary to make the social environment moral. And that can be done in only one way: by assuring the triumph of justice—that is, the complete liberty of everyone in the most perfect equality for all. Inequality of conditions and rights and the resulting lack of liberty for all is the great collective inequity begetting all individual inequities. Suppress this source of inequities and all the rest will vanish along with it.

MICHAEL BAKUNIN, *Integral Education*, 1869

A man can be truly moral only when he is his own master . . . therefore, his will cannot fail to be strengthened when he sees other men, guided like himself by their own volition, following the same line of conduct. Mutual example will soon constitute a collective code of ethics to which all may conform without effort; but the moment that orders, enforced by legal penalties, replace the personal impulses of the conscience, there is an end to morality.

ELISÉE RECLUS, *An Anarchist on Anarchy*, 1886

It is time to be finished with this fiction of the "innate" wickedness of man. It is no more true that man is "fundamentally" wicked than that he is "originally" good. The human individual is a plastic being who is what he is made to be by heredity, corrected by education, and above all, by circumstances and milieu.

JEAN GRAVE, *The Society of Nations,* 1918

Take the most intelligent ape possessing the finest character, put it under the best, most humane conditions—and you will never succeed in making a man of it. Take the most hardened criminal or a man of the poorest mind and, provided that neither suffers from some organic lesion which may bring about either idiocy or incurable madness, you will soon recognize that if the one has become a criminal and the other has not yet developed the conscious awareness of his humanity and human duties, *the fault lies not with them nor with their nature, but with the social environment in which they were born and have been developing.*

MICHAEL BAKUNIN, *Federalism, Socialism, and Anti-Theologism,* 1867

Considered from the moral point of view, Socialism is the *self-esteem of man* replacing the *divine cult;* envisaged from the scientific, practical point of view, it is the proclamation of a great principle which permeated the consciousness of the people and became the starting point for the investigation and development of positive science as well as for the revolutionary movement of the proletariat.

MICHAEL BAKUNIN, *A Member of the International Answers Mazzini,* 1871

True, real love, the expression of a mutually and equally felt need, can exist only among equals. The love of the superior for the inferior is oppression, effacement, contempt, egoism, pride, and vanity triumphant in a feeling of grandeur based upon the humiliation of the other party. And the love of the inferior for the superior is humiliation, the fears and the hopes of a slave who expects from his master either happiness or misfortune.

MICHAEL BAKUNIN, *The Knouto-Germanic Empire,* 1871

It is not love and not even sympathy upon which society is based in mankind. It is the conscience—be it only at the stage of an instinct—of human solidarity. It is the unconscious recognition of the force that is borrowed by each man from the practice of mutual aid; of the close dependency of everyone's happiness upon the happiness of all; and of the sense of justice, or equality, which brings the individual to consider the rights of every other individual as equal to his own. Upon this broad and necessary foundation, the still higher moral feelings are developed.

PETER KROPOTKIN, *Mutual Aid,* 1902

Civilized man . . . will extend his principles of solidarity to the whole human race, and even to animals.

PETER KROPOTKIN, *Anarchist Morality,* 1909

The common and basic error of all the idealists, an error which flows logically from their whole system, is to seek the basis of morality in the isolated individual, whereas it is found—and can only be found—in associated individuals.

MICHAEL BAKUNIN, *The Knouto-Germanic Empire,* 1871

Three things are necessary for men to become moral—that is, complete men in the full meaning of the word: birth under hygienic conditions; a rational and integral education accompanied by an upbringing based upon respect for work, reason, equality, and liberty; and a social environment wherein the human individual, enjoying full liberty, will be equal, in fact and by right, to all others.

Does such an environment exist? It does not. It follows, then, that it has to be created.

MICHAEL BAKUNIN, *Integral Education,* 1869

"WE ARE COMMUNISTS"

One cannot be an anarchist without being a communist. In effect, the least idea of limitation already contains in itself the germs of authoritarianism. It cannot manifest itself without immediately engendering the law, the judge, the policeman. We must be communists, because it is through communism that we will realize true equality. We must be communists because the people, who do not understand the collectivist sophisms, understand communism perfectly. . . . We must be communists because we are anarchists, because anarchy and communism are the two necessary terms of the revolution.

CARLO CAFIERO, *Anarchy and Communism,* 1880

The Revolution, we maintain, must be communist; if not, it will be drowned in blood and have to be begun all over again.

PETER KROPOTKIN, *The Conquest of Bread,* 1892

It is not everything to affirm that communism is a possible thing: we can affirm that it is necessary. Not only *can* one be a communist, but one must be one, under pain of missing the goal of the revolution.

CARLO CAFIERO, *Anarchy and Communism,* 1880

We believe that capital is the common patrimony of humanity, since it is the fruit of the collaboration of past generations with the contemporary one, and we believe that it must be at the disposition of all, in such a way that none

can be excluded from it; that no one . . . should be able to corner a part to the detriment of everyone else.
In a word, we want equality.

PETER KROPOTKIN, speech at his trial, Lyons, 1883

I am a convinced partisan of *economic and social equality* because I know that without this equality, freedom, justice, human dignity, morality, and the well-being of individuals as well as the flourishing of nations are a lie.

MICHAEL BAKUNIN, *The Paris Commune and the Notion of the State,* 1871

Communist customs and institutions are of absolute necessity for society, not only to solve economic difficulties, but also to maintain and develop social customs that bring men in contact with one another. They must be looked to for establishing such relations between men that the interest of each should be the interest of all; and this alone can unite men instead of dividing them.

PETER KROPOTKIN, *Anarchism: Its Philosophy and Ideal,* n.d.

Communism is the best basis for individual development and freedom; not that individualism which drives man to the war of each against all—this is the only one known up till now—but that which represents the full expansion of man's faculties, the superior development of what is original in him, the greatest fruitfulness of intelligence, feeling, and will.

PETER KROPOTKIN, *Anarchism: Its Philosophy and Ideal,* n.d.

The new socialized economy will be in the hands of the workers and the technicians and will have no other motive, no other end, than the satisfaction of the needs of the people. The consumer will not simply signify a market, he will not be created to purchase the products, but the products will be elaborated to satisfy his wants.

D. A. DE SANTILLAN, *After the Revolution,* 1936

If the needs of the individual are taken as the starting point of our political economy, we cannot fail to reach Communism, an organization that enables us to satisfy all needs in the most thorough and economical ways.

PETER KROPOTKIN, *The Conquest of Bread,* 1892

Socialism, as we understand, means that land and machinery shall be held in common. The production of goods shall be carried on by producing groups which shall supply the demands of the people. . . .

That is what the socialists propose. Some say it is un-American!

MICHAEL SCHWAB, on being sentenced to hang, 1886

From each according to his abilities, to each according to his needs: that is what we sincerely, energetically want; that is what will be, because there is no regulation that can prevail against claims that are at the same time legitimate and necessary.

PETER KROPOTKIN, courtroom speech, Lyons, 1883

"You said that Anarchy will secure economic equality," remarks your friend. "Does that mean equal pay for all?"

It does. Or, what amounts to the same, equal participation in the public welfare, because, as we already know, labor is social. No man can create anything all by himself, by his own efforts. Now then, if labor is social, it stands to reason that the results of it, the wealth produced, must also be social, belong to the collectivity. No person can therefore justly lay claim to the exclusive ownership of social wealth. It is to be enjoyed by all alike.

ALEXANDER BERKMAN, *What Is Communist Anarchism?* 1928

Under pain of death, human societies are forced to return to first principles: the means of production being the collective work of humanity, the product should be the collective property of the race. Individual appropriation is neither just nor serviceable. All belongs to all. All things are for all men, since all men have need of them, since all men have worked in the measure of their strength to produce them, and since it is not possible to evaluate everyone's part in the production of the world's wealth.

PETER KROPOTKIN, *The Conquest of Bread,* 1892

Who . . . can appropriate to himself the tiniest plot of ground, or the smallest building, without committing a flagrant injustice? Who, then, has the right to sell to any bidder the smallest portion of the common inheritance?

PETER KROPOTKIN, *Expropriation,* 1882

From the moral point of view, collectivization, by imposing the principle of "He who would eat must work," would give an impulse of unlimited development in the life of the people; because labor and genius would not be shut out by artificial barriers and would finally be able to convert into fact the old dream of an earthly paradise.

D. A. DE SANTILLAN, *After the Revolution,* 1936

I call myself a communist, because communism, it seems to me, is the ideal to which all mankind will aspire as love between men and an abundance of production free them from the fear of hunger and thus destroy the major obstacle to brotherhood.

ERRICO MALATESTA, *Il Risveglio,* November 31, 1929

We maintain . . . not only that Communism is a desirable state of society, but that the growing tendency of modern society is precisely toward Communism—free Communism—

notwithstanding the seemingly contradictory growth of Individualism.

PETER KROPOTKIN, *Anarchist Communism,* 1887

We are . . . anarchist communists; but this does not mean that we use communism as a panacea or dogma, and fail to see that to achieve communism certain moral and material conditions are needed which we must create.

ERRICO MALATESTA, *Pensiero e Volontà,*
August 25, 1926

Here in Fraga [a small town in Spain where anarchists had made a revolution], you can throw banknotes into the street and no one will take any notice. Rockefeller, if you were to come to Fraga with your entire bank account, you would not be able to buy a cup of coffee. Money, your God and your servant, has been abolished here, and the people are happy.

Die Soziale Revolution, Barcelona, 1937

The common possession of the instruments of labor must necessarily bring with it the enjoyment in common of the fruits of common labor.

PETER KROPOTKIN, *The Conquest of Bread,* 1892

We are communists. But our communism is not that of the authoritarian school: it is anarchist communism, communism without government, free communism. It is a synthesis of the two chief aims pursued by humanity since the dawn of its history—economic freedom and political freedom.

PETER KROPOTKIN, *Anarchist Communism,* 1887

One could easily have economic equality without having the least liberty.

CARLO CAFIERO, *Anarchy and Communism,* 1880

Those who have seriously studied the question do not deny any of the advantages of Communism, on condition, be it well understood, that Communism be perfectly free—that is to say, Anarchist. They recognize that work paid for with money, even . . . to workers' associations governed by the State, would retain the characteristics and the disadvantages of wagedom.

PETER KROPOTKIN, *The Conquest of Bread,* 1892

Communism must be voluntary, freely desired and accepted; for were it instead to be imposed, it would produce the most monstrous tyranny which would result in a return to bourgeois individualism.

ERRICO MALATESTA, *Umanità Nova,* May 15, 1920

With much reason, one could maintain that we [anarchists] are the most logical and most complete socialists since we claim for each not only his entire part of the social wealth, but also his part of the social power, that is to say, the ability to make his influence felt, as that of all others, in the administration of public affairs.

ERRICO MALATESTA and A. HAMON, Manifesto to the
Socialist Congress of London, 1896

We are convinced that freedom without Socialism is privilege and injustice, and that Socialism without freedom is slavery and brutality.

MICHAEL BAKUNIN, *Federalism, Socialism,*
and Anti-Theologism, 1867

Communism cannot be imposed from above; it could not live even for a few months if the constant and daily cooperation of all did not uphold it. It must be free.

PETER KROPOTKIN, *Anarchism: Its Philosophy*
and Ideal, n.d.

INTELLIGENT AND FREE WORK

When the man of science works and the man of work thinks, intelligent and free work will be considered a man's finest title of glory, the basis of his dignity, his right, the manifestation of his human power on the earth; and humanity will be constituted.

MICHAEL BAKUNIN, *Revolutionary Catechism,* 1865

Every animal works; it lives only by working. Man as a living being is not exempt from this necessity, which is the supreme law of life. He must work in order to maintain his existence, in order to develop in the fullness of his being.

MICHAEL BAKUNIN, *Philosophical Considerations on the Divine Phantom,* 1870

The division of labor means labeling and stamping men for life—some to slice ropes in factories, some to be foremen in a business, others to shove huge coal-baskets in a particular part of a mine; but none of them to have any idea of machinery as a whole, nor of business, nor of mines. And thereby they destroy the love of work and the capacity for invention . . .

PETER KROPOTKIN, *The Conquest of Bread,* 1892

The combination of agriculture and industry, the husbandman and the mechanic in the same individual—this is what anarchist communism will inevitably lead us to, if it starts fair with expropriation.

PETER KROPOTKIN, *The Conquest of Bread,* 1892

So long as men consider . . . manual labor a mark of inferiority, it will appear amazing to them to see an author setting his own book in type, for has he not a gymnasium or games of diversion? But when the opprobrium connected with manual labor has disappeared, when all will have to work with their hands, there being no one to do it for them, then the authors as well as their admirers will soon learn the art of handling composing sticks and type.

PETER KROPOTKIN, *The Conquest of Bread,* 1892

He who wishes for a grand piano will enter the association of musical-instrument makers. And by giving the association part of his half-day's leisure, he will soon possess the piano of his dreams.

PETER KROPOTKIN, *The Conquest of Bread,* 1892

The isolated labor of the individual mind, of all intellectual labor in the field of original research and invention but not of application, should not be paid for. But then how will men of talent, men of genius, manage to live? Of course they will live by doing manual and collective labor like all the others.

MICHAEL BAKUNIN, *The Lullers,* 1868-69

Should a professor—in a commune where it is required—concern himself solely with delivering lectures during the designated seven or eight hours, or should he concern himself as well with the preparation of the physical layout? Should he concern himself, together with the metal-worker and the mechanic, with cleaning up the dirt in the university building, and so forth? We believe that, yes, he must perform the latter task.

PETER KROPOTKIN, *Must We Occupy Ourselves . . . ?* 1873

Work will be a right and, at the same time, an obligation.

D. A. DE SANTILLAN, *After the Revolution,* 1936

With the development of education and popular culture, the slogan "He who would eat must work" has emerged as the expression of justice and freedom. All economic and social development that does not take this maxim as a basis and ideal is only a new sabotage of revolutionary action.

D. A. DE SANTILLAN, *After the Revolution,* 1936

Is it to be wondered at that folks are disgusted with work and are eager to seize any opportunity to do nothing? But when work is done under conditions fit for human beings, for a reasonable time and according to the laws of health; when the worker knows that he is working for the well being of his family and of all men; when everyone who wishes to be respected must necessarily be a worker . . . ; who will then wish to forgo the joy of knowing himself useful and beloved so that he may live in an idleness disastrous to his body and mind alike?

ERRICO MALATESTA, *A Talk About Anarchist Communism,* 1888(?)

A society whose work is free will have nothing to fear from idlers.

"But provisions will run short in a month!" our critics at once exclaim.

"So much the better," say we. It will prove that for the first time on record the people have had enough to eat.

PETER KROPOTKIN, *The Conquest of Bread,* 1892

Very often the idler is but a man to whom it is repugnant to spend all his life making the eighteenth part of a pin or the hundredth part of a watch, while he feels he has exuberant energy which he would like to expend elsewhere.

PETER KROPOTKIN, *The Conquest of Bread,* 1892

If not one of the thousands of groups of our federation will receive you, whatever their motive, if you are absolutely incapable of producing anything useful, or if you refuse to do it, then live like an isolated man or an invalid. If we are rich enough to give you the necessities of life, we shall be delighted to give them to you. You are a man, and you have the right to live. But as you wish to live under special conditions and leave the ranks, it is more than probable that you will suffer for it in your daily relations with other citizens. You will be looked upon as a ghost of bourgeois society, unless some friends of yours, discovering you to be a talent, kindly free you from all moral obligation toward society by doing all the necessary work for you.

PETER KROPOTKIN, *The Conquest of Bread*, 1892

If society were only released of the waste and expense of keeping a lazy class, and the equally great expense of the paraphernalia of protection this lazy class requires, the social tables would contain an abundance for all, including even the occasional lazy individual.

EMMA GOLDMAN, *Anarchism*, 1910

A great number of the inhabitants of the cities will have to become agriculturalists. Not in the same manner as the present peasants, who wear themselves out plowing for a wage that barely provides them with sufficient food for the year, but by following the principles of intensive agriculture, of the market gardeners, applied on a large scale by means of the best machinery that man has invented or can invent. . . . They will organize cultivation on better principles and not in the future but at once, during the revolutionary struggles, for fear of being worsted by the enemy.

PETER KROPOTKIN, *The Conquest of Bread*, 1892

The large towns as well as the villages must undertake to till the soil. We must return to what biology calls "the integration of functions"—after the division of labor, the taking up of it as a whole—this is the course followed throughout nature.

Besides, philosophy apart, the force of circumstances would

bring about this result. Let Paris see that at the end of eight months it will be running short of bread, and Paris will set to work growing wheat.

PETER KROPOTKIN, *The Conquest of Bread,* 1892

WOMEN'S EMANCIPATION

[Woman] can give suffrage or the ballot no new quality, nor can she receive anything from it that will enhance her own quality. Her development, her freedom, her independence, must come from and through herself. First, by asserting herself as a personality and not as a sex commodity. Second, by refusing the right to anyone over her body; by refusing to bear children unless she wants them; by refusing to be a servant to God, the State, society, the husband, the family, etc.; by making her life simpler, but deeper and richer. That is, by trying to learn the meaning and substance of life in all its complexities, by freeing herself from the fear of public opinion and public condemnation. Only that, and not the ballot, will set woman free, will make her a force hitherto unknown in the world, a force for real love, for peace, for harmony; a force of divine fire, of life-giving; a creator of free men and women.

EMMA GOLDMAN, *Woman Suffrage,* 1910

The right to vote, or equal civil rights, may be good demands, but true emancipation begins neither at the polls nor in the courts. It begins in woman's soul. History tells us that every oppressed class gained true liberation from its masters through its own efforts. It is necessary that woman learn that lesson, that she realize that her freedom will reach as far as her power to achieve her freedom reaches. It is, therefore, far more important for her to begin with her inner regeneration, to cut loose from the weight of prejudices, traditions, and customs.

EMMA GOLDMAN, *The Tragedy of Woman's Emancipation,* 1910

Nowhere is woman treated according to the merit of her work, but rather as a sex. It is therefore almost inevitable that she should pay for her right to exist, to keep a position in whatever line, with sex favors. Thus it is merely a question of degree whether she sells herself to one man, in or out of marriage, or to many men.

EMMA GOLDMAN, *The Traffic in Women,* 1910

The institution of marriage makes a parasite of woman, an absolute dependent. It incapacitates her for life's struggles, annihilates her social consciousness, paralyzes her imagination, and then imposes its gracious protection, which is in reality a snare, a travesty in human character.

EMMA GOLDMAN, *Marriage and Love,* 1910

We are convinced that in abolishing religious, civil, and juridical marriage, we restore life and morality to natural marriage based solely upon human respect and the freedom of two persons; a man and a woman who love each other.

MICHAEL BAKUNIN, *A Circular Letter to My Friends in Italy,* October, 1871

Marriage . . . signifies the chaining of two beings under pain of penal sanction, which implies that, short of this sanction, affection would not suffice to maintain the official family.

The cohesion of a family by force is the legal consecration of the right of reciprocal oppression.

PARAF-JAVAL, *Free Examination,* 1903

Dante's motto over Inferno applies with equal force to marriage: "Ye who enter here leave all hope behind."

EMMA GOLDMAN, *Marriage and Love,* 1910

Anarchists reject the organization of marriage. They say that two beings who love each other don't need the permission of a third to sleep together; from the moment that their will carries them there, society has no right to take note of them, and even less right to intervene.

JEAN GRAVE, *Dying Society and Anarchy*, 1893

Since the property-owning man wants to transmit the fruit of his pillaging to his descendants, woman having until now been considered as an inferior—more as a possession than as an associate—it is evident that man fashioned the family in order to assure his supremacy over woman; and for the power, at his death, to transmit his goods to his descendants, it was necessary that he make the family indissoluble.

JEAN GRAVE, *Dying Society and Anarchy*, 1893

Radical or conservative, every male wants to bind the woman to himself.

EMMA GOLDMAN, *Living My Life*, 1931

[A revolutionary] must share our conviction that woman, different from man but not inferior to him, intelligent, working, and free like him, must be declared his equal in all political and social rights; and that in free society, religious and civil marriage must be replaced by free marriage.

MICHAEL BAKUNIN, Program of the Fraternity, 1865

We demand, along with freedom, equal rights and duties for men and women.

MICHAEL BAKUNIN, Program of the Slavic Section of the International, 1872

Love being a normal function, and woman and man being called to live side by side all their lives, why envelop this organic function with mystery when it is accomplished every day under our eyes, despite the prudishness of our educators? Why shouldn't the sexes be accustomed to knowing each other from a young age, since this knowledge will be indispensable to them in orienting their lives?

JEAN GRAVE, *Bourgeois Teaching and
Bourgeois Liberty,* 1900

Love, the strongest and deepest element in all life, the harbinger of hope, of joy, of ecstasy; love, the defier of all laws, of all conventions; love, the freest, the most powerful molder of human destiny; how can such an all-compelling force be synonymous with that poor little State- and Church-begotten weed, marriage?

Free love? As if love is anything but free. Man has bought brains, but all the millions in the world have failed to buy love.

EMMA GOLDMAN, *Marriage and Love,* 1910

*ON SCIENCE, INTELLECTUALS,
AND CULTURE*

The nobility disguised its violence with divine grace. The bourgeoisie could not obtain that high patronage . . . and therefore had to seek sanctions outside of God and the Church. And it found such sanctions among the licensed intellectuals.

MICHAEL BAKUNIN, *The Lullers,* 1868-69

Culture under capitalism attains its ends through perversion and falsification in the interest of the dominating class. The public schools, the university, the cinema, the theater, sports, etc., all are used as means toward providing a legal, moral, and material foundation for the privileges of a few and the slavery of the vast majority.

D. A. DE SANTILLAN, *After the Revolution,* 1936

In their existing organization, monopolizing science and remaining thus outside of social life, the savants form a separate caste, in many respects analogous to the priesthood. Scientific abstraction is their God, living and real individuals are their victims, and they are the consecrated and official sacrificers.

MICHAEL BAKUNIN, *God and the State*, 1871

A scientific body to which the government of society had been confided would soon end by devoting itself no longer to science at all but to quite another matter, and that matter, as in the case of all established powers, would be its own eternal perpetuation by rendering the society confided to its care ever more stupid and consequently more in need of its government and direction.

MICHAEL BAKUNIN, *God and the State*, 1871

A scholar by his very nature is inclined to all sorts of intellectual and moral corruption, his main vice being the exaltation of his knowledge and his own intellect, and scorn for all the ignorant. Let him govern and he will become the most unbearable tyrant, for scholarly pride is repulsive, offensive, and more oppressive than any other kind. To be the slave of pedants—what a fate for mankind! Give them free rein and they will start performing the same experiments on human society that they now perform for the benefit of science on rabbits, cats, and dogs.

MICHAEL BAKUNIN, *Statism and Anarchy*, 1873

Let us honor the scientists on their proper merits, but let us not accord them any special privileges lest we thereby wreck their minds and morals.

MICHAEL BAKUNIN, *Statism and Anarchy*, 1873

Government by science and men of science . . . cannot fail to be impotent, ridiculous, inhuman, cruel, oppressive, exploiting, and pernicious.

MICHAEL BAKUNIN, *God and the State*, 1871

Abstraction being its [science's] very nature, it can easily conceive the principle of real and living individuality, but it can have no dealings with real and living individuals; it concerns itself with individuals in general, but not with Peter or James, not with such or such who, so far as it is concerned, do not, cannot, have any existence. Its individuals, I repeat, are only abstractions.

MICHAEL BAKUNIN, *God and the State*, 1871

Science is a weapon that can be used for good or bad ends; but science ignores completely the idea of good and evil. We are . . . Anarchists not because science tells us to be but because, among other reasons, we want everybody to be in a position to enjoy the advantages and pleasures that science procures.

ERRICO MALATESTA, *Volontà*, December 27, 1913

I do not believe in the infallibility of Science, neither in its ability to explain everything nor in its mission of regulating the conduct of Man, just as I do not believe in the infallibility of the Pope, in revealed Morality, and in the divine origins of the Holy Scriptures.

ERRICO MALATESTA, *Pensiero e Volontà,*
September 15, 1924

In a word, science is the compass of life, but it is not life itself.

MICHAEL BAKUNIN, *God and the State*, 1871

Scientism, which I reject and which, provoked and encouraged by the enthusiasm that followed the marvelous discoveries made in the field of physical chemistry and natural history, dominated minds in the second half of the last century, is the belief that science is everything and is capable of everything; it is the acceptance as definitive truths, as dogmas, of every partial discovery; it is the confusion of Science with Morals; of Force, in the mechanical sense of the word, with thought; of natural law with will. Scientism logically leads to fatalism—that is, to the denial of free will and of freedom.

ERRICO MALATESTA, *Pensiero e Volontà,*
November 1, 1924

At the present moment we no longer need to accumulate scientific truths and discoveries. The most important thing is to spread the truths already acquired, to practice them in daily life, to make of them a common inheritance. We have to order things in such wise that all humanity may be capable of assimilating and applying them; so that science, ceasing to be a luxury, becomes the basis of everyday life. Justice requires this.

PETER KROPOTKIN, *An Appeal to the Young,* 1880

The state welcomes only those forms of cultural activity that help it to maintain its power. It persecutes with implacable hatred any activity that oversteps the limits set by it and calls its existence into question.

RUDOLF ROCKER, *Nationalism and Culture,* 1933

All higher understanding, every new phase of intellectual development, every epoch-making thought, giving men new vistas for their cultural activities, has been able to prevail only through constant struggle with the authority of church and state. . . .

RUDOLF ROCKER, *Nationalism and Culture,* 1933

Culture is not created by command. It creates itself, arising spontaneously from the needs of men and their social, cooperative activity. No rules could ever command men to fashion the first tools, first use fire, invent the telescope and the steam engine, or compose the *Iliad.*

RUDOLF ROCKER, *Nationalism and Culture,* 1933

The suffocating dependence of artistic production upon wealth and patronage should cause the true artist—who is not content to produce mere marketware—to turn relentless rebel against the existing standards, to become a communist.

MAX BAGINSKI, *Mother Earth*, January, 1912

An adequate appreciation of the tremendous spread of the modern conscious social unrest cannot be gained from merely propagandistic literature. Rather, we must become conversant with the larger phases of human expression manifest in art, literature, and, above all, the modern drama—the strongest and most far-reaching interpreter of our deep-felt dissatisfaction.

EMMA GOLDMAN, *The Modern Drama*, 1910

It is sad to admit that there is a tendency in certain labor circles, even among some socialists and anarchists, to antagonize the workers against the members of the intellectual proletariat. Such an attitude is stupid and criminal, because it can only harm the growth and development of the social revolution. It was one of the fatal mistakes of the Bolsheviks during the first phases of the Russian Revolution that they deliberately set the wage-earners against the professional classes, to such an extent, indeed, that friendly cooperation became impossible.

ALEXANDER BERKMAN, *What Is Communist Anarchism?* 1928

In justice to the intellectuals, let us not forget that their best representatives have always sided with the oppressed. They have advocated liberty and emancipation, and often they were the first to voice the deepest aspirations of the toiling masses.

ALEXANDER BERKMAN, *What Is Communist Anarchism?* 1928

Even those who only *think* they are dramatists will have opportunity in a free society. If they lack real talent, they will still have other honorable professions to chose from, like shoemaking, for instance.

EMMA GOLDMAN, *Living My Life,* 1931

If music should perish in the coming world upheaval, we must risk our lives to save the Ninth Symphony.

MICHAEL BAKUNIN, comment to Richard Wagner, 1849

EDUCATION FOR FREEDOM

The strongest bulwark of the capitalistic system is the ignorance of its victims.

ADOLPH FISCHER, on being sentenced to hang, Chicago, 1886

What is education if not mental capital, the sum of the mental labor of all past generations? How can an ignorant mind, vigorous though it may be by nature, hold out in a struggle against collective mental power produced by centuries of development? That is why we often see intelligent men of the people stand in awe before educated fools.

MICHAEL BAKUNIN, *Science and the Urgent Revolutionary Task,* 1870

Governments have ever been careful to hold a high hand over the education of the people. They know better than anyone else that their power is based almost entirely on the school. Hence, they monopolize it more and more.

FRANCISCO FERRER, *The Renewed School,* 1909

The Public School! The colleges and other institutions of learning, are they not models of organization, offering the people fine opportunities for instruction? Far from it. The school, more than any other institution, is a veritable barracks, where the human mind is drilled and manipulated into submission to various social and moral spooks and thus fitted to continue our system of exploitation and oppression.

EMMA GOLDMAN, at the Congress of the Anarchist
International, Amsterdam, 1907

The modern universities of Europe, which form a sort of scientific republic, render in the present day the same services to the bourgeoisie that the Catholic Church at one time rendered to the nobility; and just as Catholicism once sanctioned the violence perpetuated by the nobility upon the people, so does the university, this church of bourgeois science, explain and legitimize the exploitation of the same people by bourgeois capital. Is it any wonder that in the great struggle of Socialism against bourgeois political economy the official science of today has decisively taken, and continues to take, the side of the bourgeoisie?

MICHAEL BAKUNIN, *Integral Education,* 1869

The professors—those modern priests of licensed political and social quackery—poison the university youth so effectively that it would take a miracle to cure them. By the time a young man is graduated from the university he has already become a full-fledged doctrinaire full of conceit and contempt for the rabble, whom he is quite ready to oppress and especially to exploit in the name of his intellectual and moral superiority. The younger such a person is, the more pernicious and reprehensible he becomes.

MICHAEL BAKUNIN, *The Lullers,* 1868-69

Only after the workers, by decades of struggle, had conquered for themselves a better standard of living could there be any talk of intellectual and cultural development among them. But it is just these aspirations of the workers that the employers view with deepest distrust. For capitalists as a class, [a] well-known saying . . . still holds good today: "We need no men who can think among the workers: what we need is beasts of toil."

RUDOLF ROCKER, *Anarcho-Syndicalism*, 1938

How to ameliorate education? How to make teaching what it ought to be? The conclusion that comes to mind is the inanity of reforms in our merchant society. For genuine reform, it would be necessary that each should act according to his tastes and according to his vocation. It would also be necessary that the children be in a favorable family or milieu. It would be necessary, in sum, to revolutionize the world.

M. PIERROT, *On Education*, 1909

Public education, not fictitious but real education, can exist only in a truly equalitarian society.

MICHAEL BAKUNIN, *A Circular Letter to My Friends in Italy*, October, 1871

As long as there are two, or several, degrees of education for the different layers of society, there will necessarily be classes—that is to say, economic and political privileges for a small number of fortunate ones, and slavery and poverty for the great majority. As members of the International Workingmen's Association we want equality, and because we want equality, we must also want complete education, equal for everybody.

But if everybody is educated, who will work? we are asked. Our answer is simple: Everybody ought to work and everybody ought to be educated.

MICHAEL BAKUNIN, *Integral Education*, 1869

The child is the property of nobody, he belongs to himself; and in the period during which he is incapable of protecting himself, when he could be exposed to exploitation, it is up to the society to protect him and guarantee him free development. The society is also charged with his maintenance: in assisting in his consumption and the various expenses his education will involve, the society is only giving an advance, which the child will reimburse to it by his work when he has become a producer.

JAMES GUILLAUME, *Ideas on Social Organisation*, 1876

The rearing of the child must become a process of liberation by methods that do not impose ready-made ideas but aid the child's natural self-unfoldment.

ALEXANDER BERKMAN, *Mother Earth*, November, 1910

In a word, our business is to imprint on the minds of children the idea that their condition in the social order will improve in proportion to their knowledge and to the strength they are able to develop; and that the era of general happiness will dawn more surely when they have discarded all religious and other superstitions that have up to the present done so much harm. On that account there are no rewards or punishments in our schools.

FRANCISCO FERRER, *The Origins and Ideal of Modern School*, 1913

Let us not be afraid to say that we want men capable of evolving endlessly, capable of destroying and renewing their environments without cessation, of renewing themselves also; men whose intellectual independence will be their greatest force, who will attach themselves to nothing, always ready to accept what is best, happy in the triumph of new ideas, aspiring to live many lives in one life. Society fears such men; therefore, we must not hope that it will ever want an education able to give them to us.

FRANCISCO FERRER, *The Origins and Ideals of the Modern School*, 1913

All rational education is at bottom nothing but the progressive immolation of authority for the benefit of freedom, the final aims of education necessarily being the development of free men imbued with a feeling of respect and love for the liberty of others.

MICHAEL BAKUNIN, *The Knouto-Germanic Empire,* 1871

We fully recognize the necessity of specialization of knowledge, but we maintain that specialization must follow general education, and that general education must be given in science and handicraft alike. To the division of society into brain-workers and manual workers we oppose the combination of both kinds of activities.

PETER KROPOTKIN, *Fields, Factories, and Workshops,* 1898

All workers ought to receive full instruction both about each specialized industry and about the whole field of industry. Thus, all large-scale industrial establishments where there is a division of functions can serve as workshop and school, both theoretical and practical, for workers who are serving an apprenticeship or who are not yet associates.

P.-J. PROUDHON, *Justice in the Revolution and the Church,* 1858

Labor, like creation itself, is one and identical in plan, but infinitely varied in the forms it takes.

Therefore, there is no reason why the apprenticeship of the workers should not be designed to embrace the whole of industrial activity instead of being simply a fragment of it.

The consequences of such a system of education would be incalculable. Quite apart from economics, there would be a profound change in the human soul; the features of humanity would be completely altered. All traces of ancient degradation would disappear, transcendental vampirism would be eliminated, the spirit would be completely changed, and civilization would move into a higher sphere. Labor would become divine; it would become the religion.

P.-J. PROUDHON, *Justice in the Revolution and the Church,* 1858

Repeating the formulation of Proudhon, we say: if a naval academy is not itself a ship with sailors who enjoy equal rights and receive a theoretical education, then it will produce not sailors but officers to supervise sailors; if a technical academy is not itself a factory, not itself a trade school, then it will produce foremen and managers and not workmen; and so on. We do not need these privileged establishments; we need neither universities nor technical academies nor naval academies created for the few; we need the hospital, the factory, the chemical plant, the ship, the productive trade school for workers, which, having become available to all, will with unimaginable speed exceed the standard of present universities and academies.

PETER KROPOTKIN, *Must We Occupy Ourselves . . . ?* 1873

Break your mental fetters, says Anarchism to man, for not until you think and judge for yourself will you get rid of the dominion of darkness, the greatest obstacle to all progress.

EMMA GOLDMAN, *Anarchism,* 1910

BIOGRAPHICAL NOTES

MIKHAIL ALEXANDROVITCH BAKUNIN, a Russian aristocrat, was born in 1814. An active revolutionary in the 1840's in Paris (where he first met, and instantly disliked, Karl Marx), Bakunin was an energetic participant in the 1848 revolution. Transferring his activities to the East, he was captured at an insurrection in Dresden, sentenced to death in two countries, and finally imprisoned in the Czar's dungeons. Exiled to Siberia, he escaped and resumed his revolutionary activity in Europe, especially in Switzerland and Italy, and participated in unsuccessful insurrections in both France and Italy. He was a member of the International Workingmen's Association (the First International) and the spokesman for the "anti-authoritarian" wing. His expulsion from the organization (and that of his close friend James Guillaume) by Karl Marx and his supporters brought about the rapid collapse of the International. Bakunin died in Switzerland in 1876.

Always on the move as a revolutionary agitator, Bakunin had neither time nor patience to complete a book, although he wrote voluminously. The only sizable work of Bakunin available in English are a compendium by the Russian Anarchist G. P. Maximoff, *The Political Philosophy of Bakunin* (London: Free Press of Glencoe, 1953), and the excellent collection edited by Sam Dolgoff, *Bakunin on Anarchy* (New York: Alfred A. Knopf, 1972). Bakunin's *God and the State* is available in a Dover Publications reprint (New York, 1970). *Michael Bakunin*, a biography by E. H. Carr, is published by Vintage Books (New York).

ALEXANDER BERKMAN was born in Vilno (then Russian Poland) in 1870 and emigrated to the United States. At the age of twenty-one, he unsuccessfully attempted to kill Henry Clay Frick, who, as Andrew Carnegie's agent, was directly responsible for the repression of the Homestead, Pennsylvania, strike. Upon his release from prison fourteen years later, Berkman resumed his Anarchist agitation, often in company with Emma Goldman. After various other spells in prison, he was deported along with Goldman to Russia in 1919. Berkman fled after the Bolshevik suppression of Kronstadt and committed suicide in France in 1936. His *Prison Memoirs of an Anarchist* are a classic of prison literature (Schocken). Of his other works, only *What Is Communist Anarchism?* is available, abridged as the *ABC of Anarchism* (London: Freedom Press, 1968).

CARLO CAFIERO, 1846–92, was a pioneer in the Italian labor movement. Although a good friend of Engels, Cafiero became a close associate and supporter of Bakunin. He spent his last years in a mental hospital, where he insisted that his window be kept closed in order not to receive more than his fair share of sunlight.

The CNT (Spanish National Confederation of Labor) was the Anarcho-syndicalist union, formed in 1910. The largest working-class organization in Spain, the CNT took over the administration of large parts of the country after the 1936 revolution. The FAI (Iberian Anarchist Federation) was a pure Anarchist organization within the labor union. Leaders of the CNT–FAI included DIEGO ABAD DE SANTILLAN, GARCIA OLIVER, and FREDERICA MONTSENY. Organizational descendants of the CNT still exist, both in exile and underground in Spain.

BUENAVENTURA DURRUTI is famous for leading the Durruti Column of Anarchist militia that fought effectively against Franco and advanced, often ruthlessly, collectivization and expropriation during its military maneuvers. Durruti was killed during the Civil War.

FRANCISCO FERRER pioneered libertarian techniques in education in Spain. He was executed in 1909 in the repression following an unsuccessful Anarchist insurrection. Ferrer's execution spurred a crisis that toppled the government. His works are unavailable in English.

EMMA GOLDMAN was born in Russia in 1869 and as a young woman emigrated to the United States. She spent the years from 1891 to her deportation in 1919 agitating for Anarchism and women's rights. Her advocacy of both led to a number of prison sentences. Exiled to Russia, she was disturbed by the progress of the revolution there and eventually fled with her close comrade-in-arms, Alexander Berkman. Goldman died in 1941 while on a speaking tour of Canada. Her available works include *Anarchism and Other Essays, Living My Life* (both Dover Publications; New York, 1969 and 1970), and *My Disillusionment in Russia* (New York: Thomas Y. Crowell, 1970). A biography of Emma Goldman, *Rebel in Paradise,* by Richard Drinnon, is published by Beacon Press (Boston, 1970).

JEAN GRAVE was a French shoemaker turned Anarchist propagandist. His book *La Societé Mourante et l'Anarchie* was banned in 1893 for its anti-militarism. Nevertheless, Grave later supported World War I and helped to split the Anarchist movement. None of his works is currently available in English.

HAYMARKET MARTYRS ALBERT PARSONS, AUGUST SPIES, ADOLPH FISCHER, GEORGE ENGEL, LOUIS LINGG, OSCAR NEEBE, MICHAEL SCHWAB, and SAMUEL FIELDEN were tried in Chicago on a charge of conspiracy after a bomb was thrown at the police during a labor rally at Haymarket Square. The first four mentioned were executed on November 11, 1887. Lingg committed suicide the day before he, too, was to be hung. The sentences of the other three were commuted after the trial was proved to have been unjust. The bomb-thrower was never definitely identified. The international holiday of May Day (May 1) commemorates the Anarchist victims. Albert Parsons' widow, LUCY PARSONS, was one of the founders of the IWW.

PETER ALEXEIEVICH KROPOTKIN was born in 1842 with the title of prince. Despite his youthful position as page to the Czar, Kropotkin's keen sense of morality led him to reject the life of a nobleman. He became a brilliant and successful geographer and finally turned to revolutionary propaganda. Imprisoned, he escaped in 1876, and became active in workers' circles in Switzerland and France (where he was also thrown in prison) and in England. Kropotkin's self-contradicting support for the Allies in World War I split the Anarchist movement. An aged veteran of the revolution, he returned to Russia after the fall of the Czar and died there in 1921.

A number of his works are available in paperback, among which the best are *Kropotkin's Revolutionary Pamphlets*, edited by Roger N. Baldwin (New York: Dover, 1970); *Selected Writings on Anarchism and Revolution*, edited by Martin A. Miller (Cambridge, Mass.: M.I.T. Press, 1970); *Memoirs of a Revolutionist* (New York: Grove Press and Dover); and *The Great French Revolution* (New York: Schocken Books, 1971). Schocken also publishes *In Russian and French Prisons;* Extending Horizons Books (Boston) publishes one of Kropotkin's scientific works, *Mutual Aid*. Benjamin Blom of New York publishes most of Kropotkin's English works in hardback, the most important of which is *The Conquest of Bread*. A biography, *The Anarchist Prince*, by George Woodcock and Ivan Avakumovic, is available, also from Schocken Books (New York, 1971).

The MAKHNOVITSI were peasants organized into a revolutionary militia during the Russian Revolution by *Nestor Ivanovich Makhno*. The Ukrainian Makhnovitsi successfully combatted both the Austro-Hungarian occupying troops and the counter-revolutionary White armies, from 1917 to 1920. The Makhnovitsi established a number of Anarchist communes, the first of which was named after the Polish-German Marxist Rosa Luxemburg. The Anarchist experiment in the Ukraine was ended when the Red Army under Trotsky turned against and finally defeated the Makhnovitsi in 1920. Makhno gloomily ended his life in exile in Paris. PETER ARCHINOV and VOLINE were members of the Makhnovitsi.

ERRICO MALATESTA was born in Italy in 1853. His career as a revolutionary began when he was expelled at age seventeen from the University of Naples and ended some sixty-odd years later, after years of prison and exile, when he died under house arrest in Mussolini's Italy. Malatesta worked as a mechanic-electrician most of his life and did not write for profit. Vernon Richard's compendium, *Malatesta: Life and Ideas* (London: Freedom Press, 1965), presents a good sampling of his newspaper articles, pamphlets, and manifestos.

PARAF-JAVAL, 1858–1942, founded an unsuccessful Anarchist "colony" in France and was an active Freemason. He was a prolific pamphleteer and an antimilitarist activist.

FERNAND PELLONTIER, 1867–1901, and EMILE POUGET, 1860–1931, were proletarian journalists and early theoreticians of French syndicalism. They were among the leaders of the labor movement at the turn of the century.

PIERRE-JOSEPH PROUDHON was born in 1809 to a French family of peasant stock. Proudhon was one of the earliest theoreticians of socialism, although he did not advocate the total abolition of private property. He was the first to call himself an Anarchist. Greatly respected by the workers of Paris, Proudhon was elected to the National Assembly after the revolution of 1848, but, feared as a revolutionary by the bourgeoisie, he was imprisoned and exiled. By the time he died in 1865, his views had become more conservative. His early work *What Is Property?*, translated by Benjamin Tucker, has been reprinted by Dover Publications (New York, 1970). Doubleday and Company publishes a compendium selected by Stewart Edwards, *Selected Writings of P.-J. Proudhon* (Garden City, N.Y., 1969). Most of his works are unavailable in English.

RUDOLF ROCKER, 1873–1958, was a bookbinder and printer who, when exiled from his native Germany, organized Jewish workers in the ghettos of London. Thrown in prison during World War I for his principled opposition to the war, Rocker returned to Germany after peace was established and organized Anarcho-syndicalist unions. He fled to the United States after Hitler's accession to power. None of his complete works is currently in print, but *Root and Branch* magazine in Cambridge, Massachusetts, plans to republish his work on *Anarcho-syndicalism*.

The WORKERS' FEDERATION OF THE DISTRICT OF COURTELARY was a Swiss workers' association within the Jura Federation, an affiliate of the Anarchist International. The 1880 program of the Courtelary workers was written by Adhémar Schwitzguébel, an engineer.

BOOKS ON ANARCHISM

Daniel Guérin's *Anarchism, from Theory to Practice* (New York: Monthly Review, 1970) is the best all-round short introduction. April Carter's *The Political Theory of Anarchism* (New York: Harper & Row, 1971) compares Anarchism to other political theories. There are unfortunately no good Marxist critiques of Anarchism; Plechanoff's *Anarchism and Socialism* (out of print) gives a highly distorted view, and a piece by Stalin is truly deplorable. Gil Green's *The New Radicalism, Anarchist or Marxist?* (New York: International Publishers, 1971) is frequently confused and inaccurate.

George Woodcock's *Anarchism, a History of Libertarian Ideas and Movements* (Cleveland: World Publishing, 1962) is the best available historical account. James Joll's *The Anarchists* (New York: Grosset & Dunlap, 1964) is also valuable, although not so extensive as Woodcock's work. *The Anarchists*, by Roderick Kedward (New York: American Heritage, 1971), contains many interesting illustrations. Paul Avrich's *The Russian Anarchists* (Princeton, N.J.: Princeton University Press, 1967) authoritatively describes the movement in that country, although Avrich devotes little space to the Makhno movement. The works that do describe that movement, Volin's *Unknown Revolution* and *Nineteen Seventeen,* are difficult to obtain, but they may be reprinted. There are no works in English devoted exclusively to Spanish Anarchism.

Obsolete Communism, the Left-Wing Alternative (New York: McGraw-Hill, 1968), by Daniel and Gabriel Cohn-Bendit, is a statement of French New Left libertarian socialism. Murray Bookchin's *Post-Scarcity Anarchism* (Berkeley, Calif.: Ramparts Press, 1971) is a stimulating application of Anarchist ideas to the modern movement. *Anarchism Today* (Garden City, N.Y.: Doubleday, 1972), edited by David E. Apter and James Joll, contains essays on contemporary Anarchist movements and includes a bibliographic essay by Nicholas Walter. Art critic and poet Herbert Read's *Anarchy and Order* (reissued by Beacon Press, Boston, 1971, with an introduction by Howard Zinn) is a collection of perceptive essays on philosophical anarchism. Robert Paul Wolff, *In Defense of Anarchism* (New York: Harper & Row, 1970), is a philosophical polemic.

A number of general anthologies are in print. Daniel Guérin's collection is by far the best, but it has appeared only in French: *Ni Dieu Ni Maître* (Paris: François Maspero, 1970). English-language anthologies include Marshall Shatz, *The Essential Works of Anarchism* (New York: Bantam Books, 1971); Irving Louis Horowitz, *The Anarchists* (New York: Dell Publishing, 1964); and Leonard Krimerman.

Readers might be interested in two anti-Statist Marxist works: *Workers' Councils* (1942), by Anton Pannekoek, and *Facing Reality* (1958), by C. L. R. James. A situationist pamphlet, *Society of the Spectacle*, by Guy Debard, attempts to assess and synthesize Marxism and Anarchism. All three works are available from Radical America, 1878 Massachusetts Avenue, Cambridge, Mass.